ABOUT THE AUTHORS

Janey Downshire and **Naella Grew** are both qualified counsellors who specialise in teenage issues and emotional literacy. They have worked together for many years designing a unique range of courses and talks which they deliver to parents, staff and teenagers through their company Teenagers Translated. This book, based on their presentations and workshops, translates current research in psychology and brain science into practical strategies for parents. As professional mothers of teenage children, Janey and Naella share many of the challenges parents of teenagers face today, and the strategies in *Teenagers Translated* are the culmination of their theoretical knowledge and direct experience.

TEENAGERS TRANSLATED

HOW TO RAISE HAPPY TEENS

JANEY DOWNSHIRE AND NAELLA GREW

Vermilion
LONDON

3 5 7 9 10 8 6 4

Published in 2014 by Vermilion, an imprint of Ebury Publishing
Ebury Publishing is a Random House Group company

The Random House Group Limited Reg. No. 954009
Addresses for companies within the Random House Group can be found at
www.randomhouse.co.uk

A CIP catalogue record for this book is available from the British Library

The Random House Group Limited supports The Forest Stewardship
Council® (FSC®), the leading international forest-certification organisation.
Our books carrying the FSC label are printed on FSC®-certified paper. FSC is
the only forest-certification scheme supported by the leading environmental
organisations, including Greenpeace. Our paper procurement policy can be
found at www.randomhouse.co.uk/environment

Designed and set by seagulls.net

Printed and bound by CPI Group (UK) Ltd, Croydon, CR0 4YY

ISBN 9780091954734

Copies are available at special rates for bulk orders. Contact the sales development
team on 020 7840 8487 for more information.

To buy books by your favourite authors and register for offers, visit
www.randomhouse.co.uk

CONTENTS

INTRODUCTION

Parenting is the most important and difficult job we ever undertake – and yet we get no training, little praise, gratitude or encouragement and no prospect of retirement. Whatever we do as parents, a certain amount of teenage turmoil is unavoidable and we need to accept that. But the passage can be smoother and this book aims to help you not only adopt a more proactive approach in order to prevent serious outbreaks of teenage antics, but also to understand how to prevent these from gathering intensity. The information is relevant to *all* parents, not only those who are struggling with problems.

The teenage years are no longer a skip and a hop from 13 to 19, so we need to reassess what we mean by this period. With children growing older younger, you may see glimpses of teenage potential in your 10-year-old. Some households may still be subsidising a child well into their twenties while they struggle to become self-supporting. This is now a much more prolonged period of parenting, possibly lasting up to 14 years, so we need to understand what is going on in this phase and to be as well prepared for it as possible.

This book aims to help raise your self-awareness – of how you *are* and what you are *doing* when in parent mode. Understanding ourselves (our reactions, responses and behaviour) helps us to develop empathy, leaving us more able to understand our child. Their culture, morality, values and beliefs about what is *normal* are different to how it was for us. Laddish drunkenness, early promiscuity, technology addiction, pornography, rebellion and depression are just some of the issues we may have to face in our families. Perhaps this sea change in what is considered to be normal is the consequence of the digital age, where the opinions and escapades of many invade our homes, altering perceptions of what is now deemed acceptable practice. Despite having been teenagers ourselves, we may feel confused about what to do and ill-equipped to do it.

A lot of what goes on with teenagers is explained by how the brain changes and develops in adolescence, so this is an important thread in the book. If we want to play a proactive part in how our child is shaping up, this book helps us look at those aspects of parenting and family life that will help us do this. Our central message is that what we do as parents matters an awful lot. The 'What can I do about their behaviour? It is out of my hands' mindset carries no weight. What we now know, through the help of research in a multitude of disciplines, is that simple everyday parenting practices can have a very positive or negative impact on a child's developing mind, personality and behaviour. Any out-of-the-ordinary behaviour is expressing an underlying need and should indicate to us that this is where we need to focus our firepower.

If our teenager's world seems confusing and out of our control, we would argue that it has never been more important for us as parents to think about what we want and what is acceptable in our own households. A set of clear, unambiguous, consistent values and boundaries at home will provide our children with the chance to develop their own moral compass. They have to learn to respect limits and adapt to different rules, be it at home, someone else's home, school, work or society as

a whole, because their behaviour impacts other people. But a familiar message reverberates around many households: 'It's so unfair, everyone else is allowed to…'. The hard thing is to hold out for what is right for your family, so not only is it a question of laying down boundaries, but also of upholding them at the risk of being unpopular with your children.

Parenting is sensitive and emotive stuff. We all want to get it right and be 'good enough parents'. Most of us take our cue from our own experience as children. Either we stick rigidly to the familiar path laid out by our own parents, or if that route did not work out well for us (too strict or too lax), or because society is very different today, we may decide to do things differently. Although our parents probably didn't think about parenting very much, the world is different now and it would be a risky strategy to cross our fingers and hope for the best. Today's problems are more complicated and require more active parental engagement and effectiveness.

Alongside this, the parent–child dynamic has undergone a seismic shift too. Adults are no longer automatically looked up to, relied upon, respected and obeyed for their wisdom and expertise. Our opinions as parents matter less and many teenage views about what is and isn't okay are moulded by their peers and the internet. Although the Web undoubtedly has huge benefits, it also plays a sinister role in a child's developing psyche by helping to challenge and modify beliefs about what is normal.

Our teenagers also live in a highly competitive world and the pressure's on. Whether intentionally or driven by fear of failure, many parents have joined the push to help their child be the best. We need to ask ourselves if our expectations are too high. Are we causing some of the problems we then struggle to manage? Have we fallen victim to the needs and wants of materialism? Reflecting on these questions, among others, will help us work out whether anything we are doing is unwittingly adding to the teenage angst in our households.

Taking risks, experimentation and pushing boundaries are part and parcel of a teenager's quest for independence. This is their last opportunity for hedonism before the dawn breaks on adult reality. As parents, we need to walk the line between not stifling their creative brain and at the same time not allowing them to reside forever in a world of make-believe. Our job is to strike the balance between allowing them freedom to spread their wings, but not implicitly sanctioning things we disapprove of because we feel we have to let them get on with it. A child without boundaries becomes headstrong and selfish so limits and guidance are vital, but we need to deliver these without micromanagement. Protecting our child from failing, making mistakes or struggling means they do not develop resilience to deal with future problems.

We know how difficult this balancing act can be as we both have teenage children (seven between the two of us). What we present in this book are the tools and responses that we have found actually work. These have been distilled over the years from our training and practise as counsellors, extensive reading from many experts who have blazed a trail before us, and from developing and conducting our range of presentations and workshops for parents, staff and teenagers around the country and overseas.

We have pulled all of this together here to give you what we hope is an informative book about teenagers. Your child may even find the chapters on habits and pastimes interesting. Throughout the book we show you *what* is going on with your teenager, *why* they do what they do and *how* you can develop strategies to deal more effectively with dilemmas when they crop up. We do this by outlining what parents need to know about the teenage brain, including how emotions impact your child's behaviour and are the building blocks of their personality. We also draw on some psychological theories to throw light on how relationships directly affect a developing teenage mind. The aim of all of this is to help you to fine-tune your relationship with your teenager and develop your own unique and effective parenting *style*.

We invite you to use this book like you would a buffet. Not everything will be relevant to your child but allow your intuition to guide you to what you might need to do *more* of and what you might need to do *less* of. Different children in your family will make distinct demands at different times. Think of this book as something that you can dip in and out of. We hope that, like our courses, it will leave you feeling optimistic and encouraged to give some of our ideas a go. Like dropping a pebble in a pond, the ripples will spread far and wide and you will find that your small changes have a big impact.

CHAPTER 1

WHAT PARENTS NEED TO KNOW

If you don't have self-awareness, if you are not able to manage your distressing emotions, if you can't have empathy and have effective relationships, then no matter how smart you are, you are not going to get very far.
Daniel Goleman, *Emotional Intelligence*

If you were asked what you think is going on in your teenager's brain, your answer might be: 'Not much!' So what exactly is going on backstage? Are all the silly things they get up to down to that vague catch-all – their hormones – or is it more than that? *The reality is that all teenage behaviour originates in the brain and the more we can understand about this the easier it becomes to work out what to do about it.* Anyone witnessing sometimes foolish or thoughtless teenage antics is surprised to find out that a huge amount of brain restructuring work is in progress during the teenage years and that it is this, plus their emotions and biochemistry, that creates the alchemy responsible for those trademark teenage behaviours. This chapter will give you a behind-the-scenes tour of how teenagers' day-to-day experiences affect their emotions, biochemistry and brain, and how this combination translates into their trademark behaviour.

WHAT'S GOING ON BEHIND THE SCENES IN YOUR TEEN?

Although the stresses of being a parent of a teenager today are probably greater than in the past, the good thing is that so much more is known about how teenagers tick and so much more is understood about how adult input influences teenage behaviour. The big change in perception goes back to the 1980s when scientists developed the use of fMRI (functional magnetic resonance imaging or neuroimaging) in order to measure the workings of a normal human brain. Now we have a clearer picture of how the brain functions, how it is structured and how it influences behaviour. In this book we use this knowledge and understanding to help you to be a more effective parent.

As a parent you may be tempted to take a fatalistic view of your children's personality traits and behaviours (e.g. shy, argumentative, depressive) – that they are inherited DNA and there is not much anyone can do other than put up with them. *When considering how much of a child's behaviour is the result of nature and how much attributable to nurture, the good news is that it is 50/50, which means that, with patience and persistence, we as parents can make changes to behaviours and even influence how our teenager's brain and personality develop.* A range of research studies over recent years specifically on the teenage brain have given today's parents hard evidence that the way you communicate with your child – those small day-to-day interactions – and family life itself have a positive and negative impact on how your child develops. The key is how we respond to teenage meltdowns and their emotional needs. If we can get our responses right we are likely to reap rewards.

Think back for a moment to when your baby was born. At birth, the cortex part of a baby's brain (the top layer of the brain responsible for thinking, see diagram on page 16) could be referred to as a 'blob of potential'. It is like a sponge waiting to soak up its nurture and adapt to fit its environment. As your baby started to get involved in her day-to-day experiences, her brain started to grow and wire itself up in its own unique way, resulting in the signature behaviours familiar to you. So, although your baby was born complete with its unique DNA blueprint with millions of genetically preprogrammed brain cells, they were all lying dormant and waiting for the powerful experience of birth and subsequent nurture to get the show on the road.

During the teenage years there is another massive burst of brain activity and reprogramming. So let's say you have noticed that your teenager has certain tendencies, for example, being anxious, stubborn or angry. Rather than seeing these behaviour habits or patterns as 100% hardwired and unchangeable DNA, visualise these habits as tracks which are developing through the experience of nurture. The more they are used, the more embedded they become – free-flowing traffic on a small track turns it into a four-lane motorway.

What brain science has now shown us is that during the teenage years there is a window of opportunity while the brain re-evaluates its existing tracks and starts to lay down its long-term paths. As a parent you can play a vital part in discouraging or deterring traffic in certain areas of teenage behaviour by the way you handle those behaviours. If, for example, you are wrestling with disrespect and rudeness and you keep responding angrily in the heat of the moment, this behaviour is likely to be fired up and gather intensity, rather than quelled, in effect making it more entrenched. Throughout this book we will make you more aware of what you need to say and how it could be said. Your responses may naturally reduce access to the rudeness or disrespect track, which will in turn become overgrown if it is seldom used. We will be addressing both preventative approaches and heat-of-the-moment ones too.

EMOTIONAL INTELLIGENCE

The other powerful new understanding relates to the role of emotions. They are to human functioning what fuel is to a car engine. Without emotions we would be stationary. We could enjoy looking at our vehicles parked outside the door, but we wouldn't be going anywhere.

Daniel Goleman's groundbreaking book *Emotional Intelligence* placed emotions in pole position on the human-functioning scoreboard, whereas until then they had been languishing, hidden under a stiff upper lip.[1]

Up until the mid-1980s, the medical model in the Western world was anchored in the view that the mind and body operated independently. Scientists viewed the brain as the control centre, directing operations and regulating human feelings, thoughts and behaviour. But where was the call to action? How come the brain just worked? What about those contained emotions brushed carefully under the carpet? What impact do they have on a personality? These were the sorts of questions that scientists have more recently sought to answer.

EUREKA! TEENAGE BEHAVIOUR EXPOSED

The new findings have made two vital contributions to our understanding. First, they showed that the internal workings of the human mind and body were inextricably connected.[2] Multitudes of studies in mind/brain and body have subsequently emerged in the last few decades (and are still emerging) providing evidence that mind, brain, emotions, hormones, genes, immunity and behaviours are all linked and work in synergy with one another.

The second important discovery was that not only is our behaviour influenced by our day-to-day experiences, but our brain also develops and adapts to fit our own unique environment.[3] How we relate, connect and communicate with important people in our lives is the most fundamental experience that we regularly undergo. Teenagers are much more sensitive than adults and tune in very quickly to what is happening around them. *In simple terms, what a teenager experiences in their environment will be reflected back in their behaviour and will become the pattern of their distinctive personality.* A stressful environment with lots of confrontation will be delivered back in combative or anxious behaviour from the teen.

UNDERSTANDING REACTIONS AND RESPONSES

When we react to an experience it is the network of our central nervous system (CNS) that communicates messages around our bodies. These internal systems, responsible for automatic bodily functions such as heart rate, blood pressure and breathing, are like a railway network. There are main-line routes with high-speed rails and peripheral networks with slower services.

KNEE-JERK REACTIONS

The body's main-line route in the CNS network links the brain and spinal cord. This network can transmit messages around the body in a matter of milliseconds and relates to survival. For instance, if you see a child about to fall into a swimming pool your body responds like lightning. The call to action – think of it like a reactor button – involves the brain's amygdala. Housed in the primitive areas of the brain it scans the world for negative, threatening experiences and it triggers our fight or flight stress response mechanism. When we sense threat we don't pause to think, we just react. The teen amygdala is highly sensitive and reads as threatening the sorts of experiences that adults might take in their stride. A simple glance at your teenager can open the floodgates. 'Why are you looking at me like that?', 'What have I done?', 'You don't like my friends/dress' and so forth.

SLOW, DELIBERATED RESPONSES

There is also a slower biochemical route that is responsible for processing feelings. When different biochemicals are triggered and released into your system you will react accordingly. For instance, if you are unhappy or sad as a result of something, you may lose your appetite, your shoulders may slump and you may look and feel depressed. This slower route does not have the same call to action as the knee-jerk reaction (see page 12).

LEARNING ABOUT SELF-REGULATION

Your internal emotional terrain changes moment to moment depending on what you are experiencing, and so it is with your teen. Imagine that you have a self-regulation dial, like the dial you might use to control your central heating. One moment you can feel quite cool, calm and relaxed (the dial may be set at three or four) and the next you can feel fear, anger, anxiety or sadness (the temperature rises to eight or nine). What is changing is the composition of your engine fuel (see page 28), which is made up of the biochemical messengers triggered when you experience something. These 'molecules of emotion' cause you to react in different ways.[4]

Let's say you are about to stand up and make a speech. Speech-making is an experience that pushes your reactor button, causing your body to release stress biochemicals such as adrenalin or cortisol. For some, making a speech is a stressful experience (say setting nine), for others it is an almost daily occurrence (maybe setting five). What happens is that your brain filters the biochemical messages it receives and adjusts your behaviour accordingly. A nine may result in a tense, hesitant delivery of your speech whereas at a five setting you would give a calm, dignified, entertaining speech. Ideally, once the experience is over your biochemistry should realign itself with the release of happy, chilled chemicals like serotonin, dopamine and oxytocin, restoring inner calm and outwardly reasonable behaviour. But teenagers have not yet established the ability to self-regulate, so they can remain pasted on the ceiling or down in the dumps for longer periods, unable to process the emotion that would help get themselves back on an even keel.

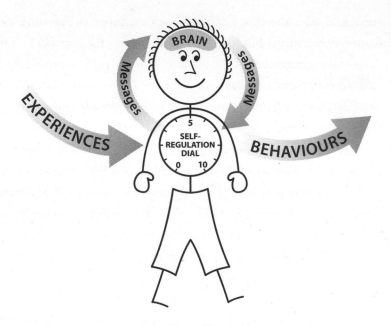

Understanding self-regulation

Different teenagers will have different thresholds of reactivity and detecting how emotions impact your teenager is a valuable tool for parents. We all react and respond emotionally to the demands of our environment, but during the period of teenage brain renovation our response system is far more sensitive and accounts for why teenagers are more over-reactive and hyper vigilant. *So a key area of our focus in this book is to show you how to help your teenager develop the ability to self-regulate their emotional turmoil and to calm their behaviour when they overreact.*

PARENT ENGAGEMENT IS ESSENTIAL

However much our teenagers may grumble about us, the fact remains that parent–child interaction represents the most significant relationship in childhood. As you move into the teenage years the ride becomes rockier, more demanding and more exhausting, but this is not the time to step back. Our parental engagement during these years is even more vital. *In this book we focus on showing you how to deliver consistent, reliable and attentive responses because these will help steady your teenager's own internal roller coaster.*

Let's think for a moment about the scale of change in a teenager. Anyone who has witnessed a boy transform during adolescence into a young man will know that the physiological alterations are momentous. Alongside these, brain transformations are under way. *The teenage years are the period when the brain undergoes its most significant overhaul, akin to a total house renovation.* Think of this change as exciting as it presents valuable opportunities to make adjustments to a previous layout or blueprint of behaviour. But it is also a vulnerable time because the brain is in a highly impressionable malleable state so that changes and habits adopted during the teenage years will steadily become hardwired and cemented in. Parental engagement helps to influence the renovations at this stage, so it is vital.

HOW THE BRAIN DIRECTS THE BEHAVIOUR ENGINE

Paul MacLean was a prominent American neuroscientist. His Triune Brain theory, the human brain is made up of three different brains and each serve a different function in behaviour, provides a useful visual picture of the internal structure and workings of a human brain (see diagram on page 16).[5] Brains 1 (primitive brain) and 2 (limbic system) are hardwired and ready for action from birth. They are concerned with keeping us alive and alerting us to threats. Brain 3 (cortex), on the other

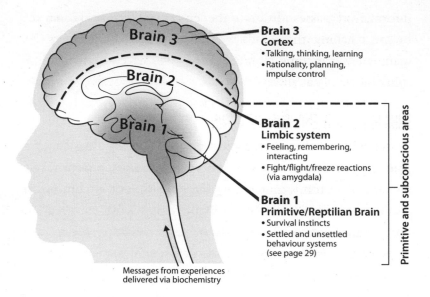

Brain 3
Cortex
• Talking, thinking, learning
• Rationality, planning,
  impulse control

Brain 2
Limbic system
• Feeling, remembering,
  interacting
• Fight/flight/freeze reactions
  (via amygdala)

Brain 1
Primitive/Reptilian Brain
• Survival instincts
• Settled and unsettled
  behaviour systems
  (see page 29)

Primitive and subconscious areas

Messages from experiences
delivered via biochemistry

The Triune Brain

hand, is softwired at birth. Your baby was born with billions of genetically pre-programmed neurons capable of making thousands of connections and pathways (their DNA). However, this process is only triggered into action as a result of external experiences (their nurture).

Think back to the speech-making example (see page 13). If you feel threatened by the experience of speech-making, the call to action will start in Brain 2. You will feel fear and anxiety, which will in turn cause the release of the stress chemicals cortisol and adrenalin. Brain 2 will process these emotional messages and Brain 3 will translate this into conscious thought – 'I hate making speeches, I'm terrified'. All this together will result in behaviour.

What we now know from fMRI scans is that bypassing or ignoring emotions (fear/anxiety) is not possible because all information passes through the emotional centre (Brain 2) before reaching the sensible rational cortex. If teenagers are completely overcome by feelings they will have a difficult time thinking clearly at all.

BEING HIJACKED BY EMOTIONAL MELTDOWN

Think back to the reactor button we referred to earlier (see page 12), which is actually your stress response system. Your teenager's button is much more sensitive than yours, but it can also feel as if your teen knows exactly how to push your reactor button and during challenging periods it may result in you feeling on permanent red alert too (see box).

EMOTIONAL HIJACKS

Red alerts are likely to feed into what Daniel Goleman called **'emotional hijacks'**. Once the limbic system is flooded with emotion it becomes uncontrollable, rather like an overloaded computer hard drive. What this does is hijack proceedings by closing the door to the logical and rational cortex (Brain 3). You know your teenager's cortex is in control when they are thinking clearly, able to make sensible decisions and control impulses like anger and frustration.

However, once in the grip of an emotional hijack your teenager is operating from their emotional limbic brain and is at the mercy of unbridled emotions. This is when we all end up saying and doing things that have not been properly thought through. Think of road rage, meltdown or seeing red to conjure up a picture of an emotional hijack.

Helping our teenagers to build a better sense of what they are feeling means they can be more aware when they are heading in the wrong direction. This might allow them a little more choice and control in how they react. Helping them to control their reactions will change their behaviour.

It is worth bearing in mind, however, that uncontained emotions are not always characterised by tantrums. One child may kick off because they are overwhelmed by feelings of irritation because they did not get their own way. Another child may be consumed by feelings of fear or shame as a result of failing, or sadness as a result of loss. In examples like these an emotional hijack may take the form of apathy, negativity, sulking, hopelessness and helplessness – the archetypal teenager slumped, moody and energy-less on the sofa. Being overwhelmed by feelings of negativity and depression can be less easy for parents to respond to effectively than those of anger or sadness.

Teenage behaviour becomes more understandable when we realise that it is the emotional Brain 2 that dominates proceedings during the teen years, because the cortex (Brain 3) is preoccupied with its overhaul and renovations (see Chapter 2). Knowing this can help us manage our own reactions better. *The teenage years are a window of opportunity because, properly handled, the renovations going on in the teen brain allow us to influence changes to behavioural pathways.* Where we can set out on the journey through the teenage years with a positive mindset, breathing optimism, excitement and hope into the family crucible, this will fuel your tanks, driving and motivating you through and around the inevitable potholes along the route. But, more importantly, this optimism will also be contagious to your child.

CHAPTER KEY POINTS

» Our personality is made up of how our brain thinks, how we feel and how we react (or behave).

» What we experience triggers emotions that activate behaviour systems in the brain.

» How we respond and interact with our teenager influences their emotions, behaviour and developing personality.

» Clear, rational, logical thinking is dependent on being able to regulate our emotions.

CHAPTER 2

THE TEENAGE EMOTIONAL ROLLER COASTER

One mustn't forget how insecure and changeable teenagers can be. One minute they're full of confidence, demanding freedom and independence and resenting all parental constraint; and the next minute collapsing into uncertainty, helplessness and demands for reassurance and support.
John Cleese and Robin Skynner,
Families and How to Survive Them

Ask most parents about when they think their child's behaviour was at its worst and most groan as they remember the challenging terrible twos with their hallmark toddler tantrums. This used to be regarded as the most significant period of brain growth, corresponding with much behavioural commotion. *What is becoming increasingly clear now is that the teen years are an even more critical period of brain development than that early growth spurt. In fact, these are the years where probably the most significant and enduring changes in our lifetime happen.*

THE TEENAGE BRAIN AND BEHAVIOUR LINK

New research into teenage highs and lows, meltdowns and histrionics, points the finger fairly and squarely at the overhaul going on in the teenage brain. With such transformative structural modifications in process, perhaps we shouldn't be surprised by the emotional roller coaster that results.

SHADES OF THE TERRIBLE TWOS?

A vital piece of new understanding is that the brain, emotions and behaviour go hand in hand. This virtually guarantees that the lengthy period of brain change from about age 11 up to age 18 in girls and 24 in boys will be accompanied by varying levels of behavioural commotion. Your previously lovely young child begins to oscillate wildly between being unpredictable, to baffling, to downright intolerable and presents you with a whole new set of parental dilemmas and another steep learning curve to scale.

TIDYING UP DIFFICULT BEHAVIOUR

Throughout childhood, difficult behaviour, unruly emotions and upsetting events have been put away in the brain's memory bank, which works like a filing system. During the teenage years, while the brain undergoes its spring clean, these old behaviour files get tossed up into the air creating mayhem in the brain. This explains why you might once again see glimpses of toddler-style behaviour from your teen.

With all these behaviour files tossed in the air the brain has some tidying up to do. In order to decide which ones get put back neatly into the filing cabinet and which get thrown out, the brain chooses to keep those behaviours that are regularly used and discards the ones that are redundant. Scientists refer to this

TENDING TO YOUR TEENAGER'S OVERGROWN GARDEN

An important point about the teenage brain is that it is very **pliable** (neuroplastic) and moulds to fit its environment.[1] This is how that process occurs. Picture your teenager's brain as a garden that has undergone a massive growth spurt and is now overrun with brambles and weeds. This is the signal for the brain to swing into action and embark on a massive tidy-up, pruning, cutting back and clearing to enable new plants to establish themselves. If these plants receive careful **nurturing** and are well tended they are likely to grow to be **strong, healthy** specimens. Think of the plants as **behaviour pathways** and bear in mind that a well-tended garden involves the little and often rule – a regular clear-out of undesirable weeds before they take root.

You also need to nourish the soil with the sort of support needed to enable your chosen plants to thrive. But unlike a garden undergoing changes, your teenager's brain modifications are more difficult to discern. Your only indication that your child's brain has started its long remarkable overhaul are the many **visible physiological changes**. Over time the brain lays down a root system that will spread far and wide during the adolescent years. Those roots, once established and mature, become significantly less malleable.

process as a 'use it or lose it' paradigm. The whole process is a little like spring-cleaning a cupboard, but because this cupboard belongs to your teenager, the actual process of managing and maintaining it is a process that can take years to fine-tune.

HOW DO YOU KNOW IT'S GOING IN THE RIGHT DIRECTION?

If all goes well, the new filing system will potentially house shiny new behaviour templates, hopefully those associated with the sorts of behaviour you would want to see in your teenager. If this is the case, you will notice:

» A growing confidence and positive attitude.
» An improvement in your teenager's attention, learning and enthusiasm in their journey.
» An improved ability to weigh up, make the right choices and decisions when facing novel experiences and pushing into unchartered territories.

When we are driven to distraction it is worth remembering that teenage behaviour is not a conscious choice, but is instead fluctuating subconscious reactions to external and internal (biochemical and hormonal) experiences. As it is a period in which behaviour patterns become established we need to remind ourselves that the more we allow a particular behaviour to be practised, the more fluent and automatic that behaviour becomes. So if, for example, we give way when a sulk reaches mammoth proportions, the child becomes increasingly proficient at rolling it out and the brain's filing system retains sulking as a useful behaviour because it is successful. The same goes for confrontation and histrionics. If your child needs to deliver an Oscar-winning performance in order to get their own way, they will continue to do so.

What can baffle parents today is that this teenage offensive seems to be starting earlier and earlier, so that today's 11-year-old might display teen behaviour more in character with that of a 15-year-old not very long ago. But don't allow yourself to be fooled. As soon as you begin to see outward physiological changes in your child, you know the brain scrambling has started.

WORK IN PROGRESS

As we looked at briefly in Chapter 1, the precise location of all the brain upheaval and change is in the cortex (Brain 3) (see page 15). Here is a quick reminder of what we know so far:

» Whereas the **primitive** and **limbic** brains (Brains 1 and 2) are **hardwired** at birth, the **cortex** (Brain 3) is **softwired** and ready to make links via our experiences.

» **The cortex is responsible for impulse control, problem-solving, decision-making and behaviour** and it does this by processing and assessing situations and comes up with a plan of action.

» **The massive growth spurt, and then the pruning back and firming up of the neural pathways, take place in Brain 3.** During this time your teenager has taken up temporary accommodation on planet emotion (Brain 2), which is making them more volatile and sensitive.

NON-VERBAL DETONATION

We've been on planet emotion before during the early years. In those preverbal days you communicated with your baby and toddler largely via non-verbal signals – eyes, touch, voice tone and facial expressions – while Brain 3 was building those initial rudimentary connections and taking tentative steps in language and logic. *During the teenage brain renovations non-verbal signals once again take centre stage.* This is why your raised eyebrow, tut-tutting or the way you look at them is enough to induce an emotional meltdown.

OVER-REACTIVITY

Much of the over-reactivity is the result of the amygdala, which is part of Brain 1 and acts like a periscope or radar, scanning the world and triggering the production of different biochemical and emotional messengers. Not only does the teen amygdala have a tendency to react in a trigger-happy way, but teenagers have also not developed the capacity for rationally processing these emotional messages, so they tend to overreact. They misread social interactions and cues, like the raised eyebrow or a sigh, and readily jump to the conclusion that you mean criticism or disapproval. Added to this, because of work in Brain 3, these predominantly emotional responses are unlikely to be mediated by logic.

WHAT PUSHES YOUR TEENAGER'S BUTTON AND CAUSES MELTDOWN?

We know that teenagers react easily to events and can struggle with regulating their emotions. We have looked at how experiences trigger the brain's behaviour pathways in Chapter 1 (see page 13). But what actually goes on behind the scenes?

Let's use the example of saying no to their request for a sleepover. This experience is picked up by your teenager's radar, pushing their reactor button. This instantly has the effect of altering their emotional regulation dial by triggering a cascade of stress chemicals into their system. This emotional fuel is processed by the brain into thoughts, which then result in a range of behaviours.

Certain experiences are virtually guaranteed to provoke undesirable reactions in teenagers. These include:

» Criticism
» Condescension
» Lack of gratitude
» Unfairness
» Being ignored
» Unrealistic goals/deadlines

However, there are plenty of other day-to-day triggers that do the job equally well:

» Fear of missing out (FOMO)
» Accepting a 'no' from parents

- » Exam performance/pressure
- » Identity/image
- » Materialism
- » Friendships
- » Troublesome relationships
- » Misunderstandings
- » Uncertainty
- » Fear of failure
- » Peer pressure
- » Choices/decisions

BIOCHEMISTRY – THE FUEL THAT STOKES THE BEHAVIOUR ENGINE

There are seven inbuilt behaviour systems housed in Brain 1 (see Triune Brain diagram page 16).[2] A simplified way of visualising these behaviour systems is to think of them as divided into two groups:

- » **Settled** (think of the good ones: care, seeking, play and sexual systems)
- » **Unsettled** (think of the troubling ones: panic, fear and rage systems)

Experiences and interactions with the world at large prompt the body to release feel-good or stress chemicals from its own in-built natural drug store. These then act like messengers, stoking the settled and unsettled behaviour systems in the brain. Think of these like muscles, regularly flexing these muscles makes them grow stronger and the ability to do or be these things grows stronger too.

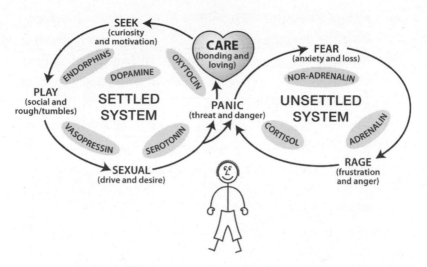

The brain's settled and unsettled systems

SETTLED SYSTEM

When everything is going smoothly as a result of positive experiences, feel-good biochemicals such as oxytocin, serotonin and dopamine are released. These leave the brain bathed in a lovely, soothing alkaline solution and result in calm, optimistic, motivated behaviour. *The longer the periods under the influence of settled chemicals, the more the brain's behaviour system learns to remain calm.*

What Fuels the Settled System?
Mrs Lovey Dovey – oxytocin
Early research attributed oxytocin with bonding and building trust. It is a feel-good chemical and is released in childbirth and breastfeeding but also by holding gentle eye contact with special people or being in a close, intimate, contented relationship. Where we respond and react to our child with undivided, calm

and measured attention at moments of crisis, this will serve to realign their self-regulation dial. Where a child's needs are met with reassuring responses the result will be feelings of warmth and calmness. Consequently your child will subliminally seek out this feeling of safety and security and will behave towards you in a more cooperative way. We can also help to maintain their feel-good chemical levels by not triggering too many stressful, anxious or overly confrontational experiences ourselves.

Mrs Happy and Joyful – serotonin

Serotonin plays a key role in moderating impulsive behaviour and is responsible for mood and overall feelings of happiness. It also helps to regulate sleep patterns by converting into melatonin. However, it is susceptible to being disrupted by the stress chemical gang. Oestrogen gets in on the act and starts to exert a bad influence on Mrs Happy and Joyful in girls aged around 11, causing a downward spiral in mood. Unbalanced serotonin levels may play a part in the onset of eating disorders (see page 122). High serotonin levels help teenagers to feel settled and under control. Experiences that promote happiness and energy trigger the body to produce more supplies.

Mrs Cool, Calm and Collected – GABA

GABA (gamma aminobutyric acid) is nature's own Valium, reducing anxiety and promoting inner peace by turning off adrenalin supplies and calming us down. It is also a necessary building block in order that the body can manufacture endorphins and serotonin. Without it we will be anxious, suffer from depression and have problems sleeping. It is available as a supplement.

Mr Motivated – dopamine

Dopamine is responsible for brain growth, motivation, enthusiasm, energy, curiosity, sexual drive, ambition and engagement in learning. It is the optimum fuel in the tank and the wonder drug for teenagers. Dopamine plays a huge part in focusing and attention. It is also the key to understanding addiction (see Chapters 5 and 6).

Mr Pain-free and Feeling Goooood – endorphins

Like the body's own analgesics and antidepressants, endorphins are responsible for reducing pain, stress levels and negative feelings about ourselves, producing instead feelings of well-being. They are produced during exercise, excitement, love and orgasm, and in response to – and in order to counteract – pain. They have been described as a morphine-like substance produced by the body.

Mr Fun and Games – vasopressin

There is evidence that vasopressin plays an important role in social behaviour, sexual motivation and bonding. In terms of good bonding, vasopressin is produced in small children's brains (from around nine months) as a result of rough and tumble play with parents. Establishing optimum levels of Mr Fun and Games results in boys being less aggressive and therefore resulting in better social behaviour, friendships and relationships.

UNSETTLED SYSTEM

The central chemicals powering the unsettled system are adrenalin, noradrenalin and cortisol. *While these play a vital role in preparing us for an emergency, performance, exam, etc., if the body's levels remain locked at high after the need is over, this results in an unduly stressed child who will be prone to over-reactivity.*

Negative experiences will tip your teenager into their unsettled system because they are read as threatening by the overzealous teenage amygdala. As a result of panic, stress chemicals such as cortisol are released into the system and leave the brain bathed in an acid solution. This is the emotional hijack we talked about in Chapter 1 (see page 17). We will all have experienced the resulting bull-in-a-china-shop reaction expressing anger and frustration; or the headless-chicken response showing panic and fear; or the rabbit-caught-in-the-headlights reaction betraying apathy.

The more frequently the stress chemicals are introduced into the brain's behaviour system, the more unsettled behaviour is exercised.

If your teenager slips easily into unsettled and difficult behaviours, all is not lost. The teenage brain changes provide a window of opportunity for kick-starting key positive biochemical activity via positive experiences in order to trigger these good biochemicals to more frequently activate the settled system.

What Fuels the Unsettled System?
Mr Bad Boy Stress – cortisol

The body produces cortisol first thing in the morning, so if someone is a stress merchant anyway mornings will leave them feeling even worse, perhaps even nauseous. Food and water will help alleviate some of these symptoms. Bear this in mind particularly when you wake your child up for school or after they have overdone things on a big night out. Having consistently high levels of cortisol can be a key player in developing mental illness and decreased resilience during the teenage years. Like adrenalin, cortisol plays a part in the fight/flight/freeze stress response (see page 12), but it needs to find an outlet so that the body can return to business as usual. Think of some of the difficult behaviour you see as a natural physiological response to trying to let off steam. Otherwise cortisol builds up in the system, becoming anxiety or stress.

Mr Fight and Flight – adrenalin

Manufactured from dopamine, this get-up-and-go chemical is responsible for getting you pumped up and kick-starting the heart to race into action. Optimum levels of adrenalin are a good thing, sharpening the senses and improving performance. However, it can have a tendency to boil over into a fight/flight/freeze stress response causing an emotional hijack of the brain. If levels remain high they interfere with the ability to concentrate and the racing heart plays havoc with sleep patterns, levels of irritation and behaviour. Supplies of adrenalin can fall when dopamine levels rocket and then plummet after big nights out, resulting in a massive slump in motivation and energy.

Mrs Anti-depression – noradrenalin

Similar to adrenalin, noradrenalin is produced by the body, but it can also be administered for depression along with serotonin because it causes a reaction in the brain positively affecting mood and behaviour.

What About Hormones?

In addition to these chemicals there are also hormones that gather momentum and intensify as a child approaches puberty. They conspire to impact on behaviour even more. Two important behaviour-related hormones are testosterone and oestrogen.

Big Mr Testosterone

This is the male sex hormone, high levels of which will result in confidence and a drive to win. It also plays a part in male behaviours like dominance, impulsiveness and play fighting, and very high levels can easily tip over into aggression. Testosterone fluctuations might result in other behaviours like defensiveness, not showing weakness, hostility and also sometimes difficulty in holding eye contact or showing care (for example, to siblings). Testosterone levels are particularly trigger-happy during the teenage years and are adversely affected by lifestyle choices (such as alcohol, cigarettes, sedentary activities). Low levels can lead to low libido or depression.

Miss Sexy Oestrogen

The female sex hormones rise during puberty and are responsible for female characteristics, sex drive and reproduction. Like testosterone, levels can fluctuate as a result of lifestyle. For example poor diet, excessive exercise or the contraceptive pill or implants can result in hormonal shifts and could result in depression and moodiness.

BRAINS: MALENESS AND FEMALENESS

The maleness or femaleness of the brain is thought to be down to varying levels of testosterone at birth. Some girls can have fairly high levels of testosterone, making their brains a little more like those of boys.[3] As a result these girls may find certain male skills, such as navigating or abstract reasoning, a little easier. The information in the table below may help you to better understand and support your teenagers' differences.

USEFUL FACTS ABOUT MALE AND FEMALE BRAINS

Brain functions	Boys	Girls
The hare (girl's brain) and the tortoise (boy's brain)	Male brain takes much longer to reach full maturity – around age 24 – allowing a longer window of opportunity for parents to exert an influence	Female brain renovations are complete around the age of 18, enabling girls to move back into their newly refurbished, thoughtful, rational brain
Right-hand side (RHS) – primitive/ emotional; left-hand side (LHS) – logical/ language	Boys only use the RHS to assess experiences, so are more likely to be reactive and negative	Girls use both RHS and LHS when assessing situations, enabling better self-control and management
Bridge between emotional right (RHS) and chatty left (LHS)	The bridge that separates the two sides allows less traffic to move from RHS to LHS in the male brain, resulting in boys talking less	Girls are wired up with a freer flow between the RHS and the LHS, giving them the ability to talk about emotional ups and downs
Managing and processing emotion	Overwhelmingly negative emotions stay locked in the RHS leaving boys vulnerable to detonation. They often don't know what they feel, so assessing their own emotional state is harder and they need more space and time to do so	Girls find recognising, understanding and controlling their emotions easier because they are less reactive and are able to process and therefore diffuse stressful emotions

Brain functions	Boys	Girls
Expressing and articulating	Less traffic from RHS to LHS and managing more negative emotions results in difficulties in expression and articulation. Not talking is less about not wanting to and more about not being able to. Hence grunts and minimal communication	More free-flowing traffic between RHS and LHS and being able to socialise allows girls the opportunity to vent and discuss feelings. This helps them to be more objective and have higher levels of emotional intelligence
Sleepyhead!	A male brain can have a tendency to daydream, be sleepy or seem to be lazy. Lethargy may be grounded in fear/uncertainty (or the result of overindulgence). Risky, physical and exciting activities – not sedentary sofa ones – provide the right stimulation and wake-up call	Girls have fewer attention and lethargy issues than boys, but to optimise focus and concentration and minimize stress, they too benefit from interspersing working/revising with short bursts of physical activity or getting outdoors
Taking risks	The male brain gets excited by risk, competition and danger resulting in much-needed dopamine and get-up-and-go. However, overexcitement shuts the door to sound judgement, self-control and the ability to see negative consequences	Facing risks and challenges triggers fear (stress chemicals), leaving girls feeling nauseous. More exposure with stepping outside comfort zones and giving things a go will improve side effects. Girls' tendency to caution works as a natural brake pedal allowing them to weigh up consequences

Brain functions	Boys	Girls
Stress	Fires up the male brain with excitement and thrill at the prospect of the chase, leaving them sharp and focused on the action, hunter-gatherer style. They are accelerator driven but overexcitement may result in trouble	The female brain is primed to focus on survival and danger. Girls worry and ruminate about what might go wrong and this sometimes leads to paralysis in making decisions. They don't understand ill-thought-out male antics
Making mistakes	Boys assess mistakes via the negative RHS of the brain. Looking a fool, failing to achieve and getting things wrong can result in toxic shame, anger or fear, resulting in aggression or doom and gloom behaviour	Girls are more able to reflect, talk things through and decide on a different tack for next time
Linking actions to consequences	This is the final piece of the jigsaw to drop into place aged 24. Boys need time to discuss pros and cons in order to develop the art of accountability and consideration	When faced with risk, the cautionary part of the brain lights up – 'If I do this, then that will happen', naturally setting girls up for protecting, caring and nurturing

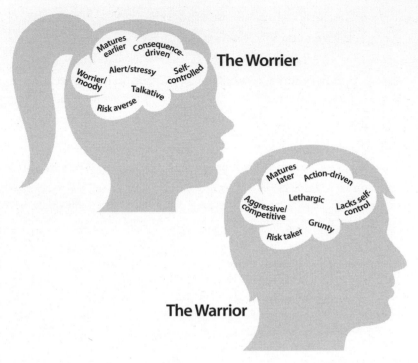

The Worrier

Matures earlier

Consequence-driven

Worrier/moody

Alert/stressy

Self-controlled

Talkative

Risk averse

The Warrior

Matures later

Action-driven

Aggressive/competitive

Lethargic

Lacks self-control

Grunty

Risk taker

Male and female brains

IS EVERYTHING OKAY ... OR NOT OKAY WITH YOUR TEENAGER?

The teenage years are a difficult time and we now have a lot more information on why that is so. Multidisciplinary research over the past decade in areas of neuroscience, biochemistry and psychology points to new understanding that during the teen years:

» Emotions are firmly occupying the driving seat.
» The trigger-happy amygdala is prone to overreaction.
» A multitude of day-to-day experiences and interactions provoke flood warnings in the emotional Brain 2.

» The cortex (Brain 3) is still developing the art of self-control and emotional containment.

» Day-to-day experiences (internal and external) allow unsupervised access to the body's natural drug store.

All this results in many physiological reasons why it is normal for teenagers to vacillate, to some extent, between being okay (settled system) and not okay (unsettled system). *What we want to avoid is to have them endlessly stuck in their unsettled system, or oscillating wildly between the two and producing behaviours that are difficult to handle or change.*

BEING EMOTIONALLY ADEPT

In today's world it is rare that we are faced with life-threatening situations. Today's stress normally comes in the form of work, family, relationships or financial difficulties, leaving us feeling okay or not okay.

When asked about what they feel, most teenagers come up with 'Great' or 'Rubbish' and are always surprised when they are told that there are over 5,000 feeling words in the dictionary! Helping teens to recognise what they are actually feeling and to articulate it with an accurate word is an important step in helping them to process their emotions. Unprocessed emotions result in protracted periods in the unsettled system, so it is important that they learn the skill of bouncing back when hurt or upset.

The feelings wheel is a good tool to help develop a more nuanced sense of your teenager's emotional state. It also helps teens to identify where they are at a given time.

It is broadly divided into settled and unsettled feelings and behaviours. The wheel starts with primary feelings – which start as an internal state – at the core and fans into a multitude of

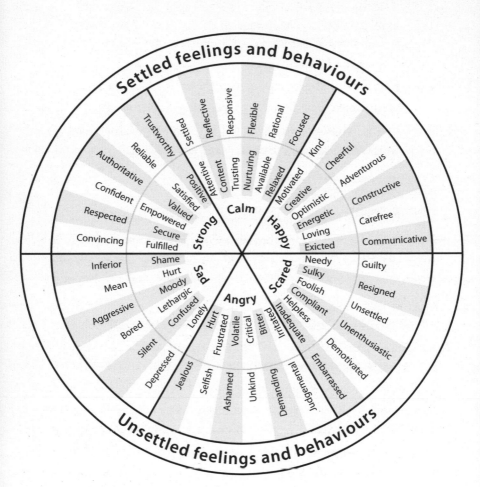

The feelings wheel

exterior emotional and behavioural states towards the perimeter. This helps us work out what is going on with our teenager. For example:

» **Being bored, lethargic or negative** may signal that they are **sad or confused**.
» **Being foolish, sulky or needy** may be a mask for **being scared of failure or feeling inadequate**.
» **Being demanding, selfish or unkind** may be **concealing anger** (at themselves or others).

UNDERSTANDING AND MANAGING NEGATIVE FEELINGS

There are good reasons why we are all equipped with both negative and positive feeling states and the more we can help our teens realise that both these sets of feelings are normal, the easier they will find it to acknowledge, process and get beyond the negative ones. Problems arise when we try and ignore the negatives, which means they build up a head of steam that eventually expresses itself in a destructive way.

Negative feelings associated with an unsettled state (scared, angry, sad) can be useful if they are constructively harnessed to action change. Whether or not this is possible will depend largely on the extent and depth of the emotion, what has triggered it, how long it has been present and whether it has been expressed. The right amount of fear (adrenalin) in a performance situation is a crucial motivator, and the right amount of anger can help to assert needs in a constructive way. However, too much of these emotions would be damaging and counterproductive in these scenarios.

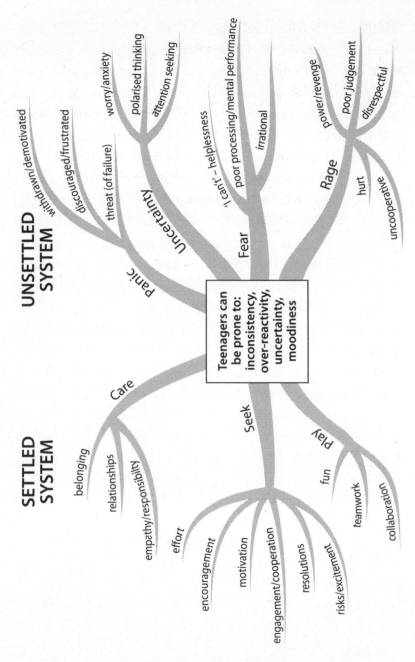

Settled and unsettled behaviours

SPOTTING SIGNS OF A NEGATIVE MINDSET

Negative emotions will not only trigger behaviours associated with the brain's unsettled system, but they will also affect how the mind works and the quality of thoughts. At the best of times, teenagers have a tendency towards negativity that is often characterised by polarised thinking and black-and-white language. Drama-queen style overreactions to ordinary events or a tendency towards misreading and misinterpreting situations are a sign that your teenager may be stuck in their unsettled system. It is worth listening closely and tuning in to their vocabulary. Are they often using words like should, ought and must? Or do they easily spiral into a doom-and-gloom appraisal: 'I never…', 'It will be like this forever…', 'I can't…', 'It won't happen…', 'There's no point…'.

The emotional and behaviour systems housed in the primitive areas of the brain are evidenced by the visible behaviours we see. These may be communicated verbally or non-verbally. During the teenage years it is normal to see a child move in and out of panic, uncertainty, fear and rage. However, we need to see plenty of evidence that they are in their settled system too, for instance by seeing them develop good friendships, demonstrate motivation, show optimism and excitement about life and have a varied set of interests.

CHAPTER KEY POINTS

» The brain undergoes a complete overhaul in the teenage years. During this time, teens are functioning more from their emotional brain.

» While emotions are in the driving seat, teenagers are highly sensitive and tend to overreact to experiences.

» During the uncertainty and upheaval of growing up, teenagers are likely to exhibit behavioural ups and downs as a result of yo-yoing biochemicals and hormones.

» Understanding what is going on and how feelings affect teenage behaviour and thinking gives parents a chance to help teenagers better manage these settled/unsettled behaviour highs and lows.

CHAPTER 3

DEVELOPING PARENTING HABITS AND SKILLS

When people think that parenting comes naturally, they are correct ... but it comes naturally the way you learned it, it doesn't necessarily come naturally to do it differently.
Roy Muir, professor of psychiatry

In today's complicated world teenagers face more stresses than we could ever have imagined at their age, and it is easy for us as parents to feel deskilled, bewildered and uncertain about what to do. More likely than not our blueprint for how to parent will have come from our own experience of childhood and few of us will either want to reject this wholesale or copy its every detail. In many respects, parents and their children are pioneers moving into previously unexplored territory, unable to decipher the path ahead. This is where an awareness of what makes us and our children tick is key in building our confidence and helping us accurately assess what is going on, and making effective choices in how to respond. *This chapter will help you identify how to gauge the emotional terrain of you and your teenager and will point to skills and practical tips that will help you get through challenging situations.*

BUILDING PARENT SELF-AWARENESS

Parenting is a journey and the teenage years can feel like driving on badly lit and poorly signposted roads. It is a time when some parents may encounter serious problems with their teenager ranging from depression, substance abuse, addiction, internet influence and risky self-harming behaviour, to name a few. Other parents might have a slightly easier time, but will still be struggling with teenagers who are growing, changing and stretching the limits in a way that will be stressful and will inevitably push buttons.

GETTING TO KNOW YOURSELF AS A PARENT

Being an autopilot parent means you will keep falling into the same dysfunctional patterns of reacting when issues come up. This will mean nothing changes. Working out what causes you to react will help you to find the button on your self-regulation dial so that you can control it yourself rather than have your teenager (or anyone else's) finger glued to it. Knowing how you tend to respond when stressed shines a light on the way ahead, offering you choice in how you react. Gauging whether you overreact (become manic/angry) or under-react (become detached/ignore them) when you hit a rough patch provides the opportunity to fine-tune your responses.

A sobering thing to remember is that your teenager's own way of reacting is being learnt from emulating you.

COUNTER-INTUITIVE PARENTING SKILLS

When your teenager is not okay, as a parent you are likely to go into autopilot care mode because you are biologically programmed to rescue, to swoop them up in your arms and to kiss it better. Well-meaning attempts to help a child avoid pitfalls and to ensure that their journey is trouble free will mean that your teenager does not experience disappointment and therefore does not learn how to bounce back from bad times. Resilience is the art of being able to bounce back and forth between feeling not okay and getting back on track. Like a muscle, resilience needs practice and exercise to improve its suppleness and elasticity.

It may feel counter-intuitive or mean to stand by and let them fail/suffer disappointment/feel ashamed, but you are in effect handing them the opportunity to develop their own strategies to cope with negative experiences. It will help them fine-tune their early-warning system, which will alert them to avoid similar situations in the future and manage difficult times later in their life. The better they get at this, the more quickly they will be able to cross the bridge from being in an unsettled to a settled mindset. The parent who rescues and hovers when panic kicks in (due to some drama/challenge) ensures that their child hands over responsibility while they take charge of the controls. This scenario may mean that as teenagers inevitably turn their attention towards their peers, the risk is that they become unduly influenced by undesirable peer pressure.

How often have you thought 'Should I let them?', 'What if x happens?', 'Is this the right time to let them?'. *The difficult balance is to demonstrate that you care and that you are there for them, but that you are now holding back and letting them tackle challenges in the knowledge that you are there as a safety net if they need you.*

KNOWING WHEN AND HOW TO DELIVER APPROPRIATE HELP

When things do go wrong, which they will, teenagers need to know where the help and support is. Your 17-year-old is less likely to want to run and sit on your knee, but the need for reassurance and a sense of belonging is still the underlying emotional need when the proverbial hits the fan.

Attention, time and care work best when they are drip-fed when required. Moments of bonding demonstrate care and affection. Boys need shoulder-to-shoulder bonding, such as doing fun things together and talking in the car so they can process and build awareness. Then if they are away from home and things go wrong, a chance to talk and hear your reassuring, familiar voice may be enough to smooth ruffled feathers. If a parent steps too close brandishing pity and sympathy, or their own neediness, they may get rebuffed. A parent acting hurt and upset will further compound unsettled anger. A parent needs to exhibit anchored, calm, no-nonsense reactions in order to teach and develop the capacity for self-control. Girls can be needier, but they are better equipped to get those needs met because their ability to talk about their problems helps to dissipate their concerns.

EMPATHIC PARENTING

Empathy is a useful parenting skill in understanding the teenage world and helps us contain our reactions. Infuriating as teenagers may sometimes be, if we parents can step into their shoes from time to time and see life through their eyes we will find it easier to modify our own responses. It is a confusing and emotionally volatile phase. Your teen may look like an adult and want the freedoms of an adult, however, 24 hours in the company of the average teenager reminds us that they are still children in many ways, plus they find it harder to express their needs. They still need our attention, time and nurturance, but will often reject it if it is offered in the wrong way for them. What works for one teenager doesn't for another and this is where empathy helps us in tuning in to what is bothering them and providing them with the emotional responses that they need. When we get the balance of engagement right, this results in everyone feeling more optimistic and confident, which in turn feeds into a calmer and less reactive atmosphere at home.

UNDERSTANDING HOW YOUR REACTOR BUTTON LINKS TO YOUR VALUES

Empathy is hard to muster when your button has been pushed. The sorts of things that will instantly achieve this and send your inner emotions into pandemonium are when your own values are threatened.

So what are your buttons – those issues over which you can be relied upon to ignite? Those areas where your teenager only needs to light the fuse and then they can sit back, relax and enjoy the show. Take a few minutes to think about what really matters or is of value to you in life because these will be closely linked to what sets you off. Values are an intensely felt and personal thing for us all, developed over a lifetime and powerfully influenced by our own childhood and the rules we imbibed from our parents during those early years. They have become our principles and we will take a firm line in order to uphold them.

So if, for example, you feel strongly about honesty, being spun a lie by your teenager is going to be particularly incendiary for you. For someone else the same strength of reaction might be elicited by laziness if a good work ethic happens to be one of your core values. Alternatively swearing may set you off if you never used bad language to your parents when you were younger. *It is a good idea, therefore, to reflect on what attitudes, behaviours and innate qualities you feel strongly about so that you know the issues over which you are most likely to react.*

MAKE A LIST

List the **principles, attitudes and behaviours** that are important to you. Put them in order of importance and review the list from time to time. It might be punctuality, table manners, respect for older people, cooperation, kindness, effort, self-discipline...

Button Pushers and Detonation

Being sure of your own principles and values is helpful because they are driving your reactions and responses. Try to develop a better awareness by assessing:

» Which ones really set you off?
» How do you react when pushed?
» Which child pushes which button?

Forewarned is forearmed. You may realise that as they get older, some of their new choices like tattoos, casual sex or binge drinking also provoke you, so work out how you react when pushed. For instance, some people detonate, while others quietly seethe.

Knowing all this gives you an early-warning system that indicates what might lie ahead. It also allows you to tackle – at a time when you are feeling calm and relaxed – those emotive issues that you know are guaranteed to cause a family rumpus. This gives your child a chance to know where you stand and talk to you about their opinions should they be at odds with yours, generating discussion. This also allows you to see how your teenager's thinking is developing so they can reflect on the potential consequences of their actions should they decide to follow their instincts regardless of your reservations.

So when your teenager steps too close to the boundary, if you know where you could be heading you will be able to remain more calmly anchored.

FLEXIBILITY AND ADAPTABILITY

A lot of skirmishes between parents and teens seem to take place over the issue of developing attitudes. These don't really feature in the early years, but as your small and relatively pliable child goes through the long transition period of adolescence and transforms into an independent adult, your own personal attitudes and values may have to be modified. Household rules that worked well for toddlers are likely to need adapting to accommodate a family of grown-ups. Some of the values with which our generation was raised, for instance, may not hold sway with today's teenagers and will require updating and negotiation. For example: 'Children should be seen and not heard', 'No sex before marriage', 'Only speak when spoken to'.

If this wasn't taxing enough, the teen years also demand that we change tack in how we take a stand on predictable issues, such as their taste in clothes, tidiness, when they get up, organisation, hygiene, friendships and working methods. Fighting through the mounds of washing in their room or finding them still in bed at midday tests restraint to the hilt. However, you can protect yourself by developing a more flexible attitude when they are in their own space, for example, their bedroom. If they perceive some flexibility from you over some issues they are more likely to toe the line over those non-negotiable areas.

Where we may be willing to compromise on some of these issues now our child is growing up, there may be non-negotiable areas, for instance manners, kindness and teenage sex. Sometimes, we may just expect our children to know what we feel, but teenagers are not renowned for their powers of perception and they need to have our values spelt out to them in a calm and firm way. Both parents may also have distinct values or may prioritise the same set of values differently, so children need to learn to respect both sides.

BOUNDARIES WITHIN BOUNDARIES

You may decide to relinquish control over something like bedroom tidiness as it is lower down on your list of rules – living in a pigsty is their choice – but spreading their untidiness around your house may be beyond what you can tolerate. Alternatively, you may take a more relaxed line on tracksuits and trainers for tea with granny, provided they are polite and helpful and not continually checking Instagram. Explaining this so that they can see where you can be flexible and where you can't helps them learn how to **negotiate** and **bold cooperate**. While they are doing this, they are also imbibing what matters to you and developing their own **inner conscience and moral compass.**

This will help them to:
» Distinguish right from wrong.
» Weigh up and make balanced choices.
» Be reliable and do what they say they will do.

KNOWING WHERE YOU STAND

Knowing where you stand, and respecting that, is a crucial part of your teenager learning to recognise and observe limits and no-go areas. Boundaries represent part of the secure wall that children need to feel around them. However much they may object, boundaries are like a pair of strong invisible arms that make them feel safe. The world outside your family offers porous and often contradictory boundaries that are confusing for teenagers. Envisage your family as its own micro society, equipped with its own idiosyncratic guidelines that offer your child security and clarity. With this in mind, make a note of the most important boundaries you want to uphold. *Keep your rules simple, clear and logical. This makes them easy to impose and easy to comply with.*

STRESS = REACTIONS + RESPONSES

Being told we are on a short fuse is just about guaranteed to put already high stress levels through the roof. Quite a lot of what goes wrong between parents and teens is the result of stress – ours and theirs. Our children absorb ours, which has the effect of amplifying theirs, and vice versa. What starts out as perhaps a work-related stressor very quickly starts contaminating the home environment. It can be helpful to take a moment to think about what else is going on in life other than trying to manage teenagers, so that you can gauge where you might be on the stress scale. Separating out independent tensions from child-related ones helps keep things in perspective.

Stress is about how we react emotionally and physiologically to life's challenges, and how we behave as a result. It goes hand in hand with anxiety, panic and depression, so identifying the downward spiral in the early stages is crucial in order to stop the slide. Equally important is realising that the button pushers we have been looking at are the issues most likely to cause the highest intensity of stress.

GOOD STRESS

A certain amount of stress is not only inevitable but also helpful. This good stress is when your body reacts to a threat/pressure/challenge and you respond in ways that are appropriate to the provocation. So, for instance, if you have a race to run or an exam to sit, a certain amount of pressure and threat will promote a surge of adrenalin and cortisol, getting you ready for action. What happens is that your self-regulation dial moves from a setting of say three up to seven/eight. This is the body's primitive call-to-action system that works to marshal the troops. Provocation from your teenager – say rudeness or selfishness – will have a similar effect. What makes this a normal stress reaction is that your response is appropriate to the event. This is okay provided you don't overreact and your body's biochemistry realigns itself after the event, bringing your self-regulation dial back down to a three setting where inner calm is restored.

BAD STRESS

From time to time we all hit a rough patch when the stress regulator doesn't work quite so well and events and circumstances are so challenging and relentless that your dial remains stuck at a setting of five/six. What makes stress bad is that it is akin to leaving your car engine running 24/7, even when parked, resulting eventually in engine burnout. Often this can happen when life experiences become out of kilter with, for example, ongoing problems at work, in our marriage, finances or health. Most of us know that at these times we feel emotionally exhausted and our tolerance thresholds to other

WHAT ARE THE SIGNS OF BAD STRESS?

Being aware of some of the signs will help you distinguish bad stress from good.

» **Poor tolerance of small incidents and people** – a tiny spider across the sensor is enough to trigger your internal alarm system.

» **Feeling close to meltdown as if you are only just holding it together** – emotions (tears?) keep bubbling up to the surface ready to hijack proceedings.

» **Other seemingly unrelated things keep going wrong and adding to your angst** – everything seems to be tarred with the same brush.

» **Close relationships are suffering** – interactions with teenagers escalate into confrontation and battles.

» **Insomnia** – problems getting to sleep, waking in the night, waking too early; the body and mind are on red alert and poised for action 24/7.

» **Bad dreams** – as if the brain is busy trying to tidy up the emotional fallout from life's events.

» **Tired all the time** – as a result of sleep interruption and whirring stress hormones.

» **Illness and pain** – an alerted stress system puts your immune system on hold.

» **Need for coping strategies** – e.g. a drink or a cigarette, in order to calm frazzled nerves.

triggers, such as our teenager, are likely to be low. A spilt drink on the carpet or a bedroom bombsite will cause you to detonate and overreact. This can be a time when we feel vulnerable on many levels.

THE POWER OF CALM

So how do we begin to restore calm? As we looked at in Chapter 1, Brain 1 (primitive brain) and Brain 2 (emotional brain) are functioning subconsciously and out of awareness. Learning how to recognise what is impacting these two brain areas, and how you respond as a result, will improve your self-control. Awareness requires being conscious of the triggers that set you off; knowing the intensity with which you respond; accepting that there is a problem that needs managing; and learning and practising how to soothe and calm yourself so you can approach the issue in a proactive way.

Here is how you might do this if, for example, you are trying to avoid further drama with your teenager:

> » **Be open and communicate how you are feeling.** If your child is aware that you are feeling stressed they will begin to understand that your tolerance levels will be lower and you arc morc likcly to detonate. This helps them start to take responsibility and choose how best to negotiate the potential landmines. This is something that will hold them in good stead in later life as they will be more sensitive to reading the emotional state of those around them.
> » **Become more emotionally savvy.** Be aware of how you feel in the early stages of a meltdown in order to be able to take control of the situation before things

have begun to spiral out of control. Choose to respond to teenage demands when you are aware that Brain 3 (cortex) is in the driving seat. Explain that you will deal with their request later.

» **Give yourself time to react appropriately.** Six seconds gives enough time to start to realign stress chemicals and gather some self-control in order to choose when and how you want to respond and what you would like to say. While your child is emotionally darting around, picture yourself firmly anchored in order to bring them back to earth by remembering that:
  • (Your) **confrontation** escalates (their) **tension**.
  • (Your) **tension** raises (their) **anxiety** levels.
  • (Your) **fear** fuels (their) **aggression**.

» **If you do overreact or say the wrong thing in the heat of the moment, apologise for the specific issue that you feel sorry about.** E.g. 'I should not have spoken to you in that way at that time.' This will nip the tiff in the bud and also demonstrate the art and value of apologising.

» **Avoid getting hooked into the fault/blame game** ('It's all your fault, you made me'). This will simply prolong the fracas for several days.

Horse Whispering

Tethering ourselves when overwrought is not easy, but it is possible to train yourself to hold your horses, or at least to reduce your levels of anxiety. The more your teenager watches you do this successfully, the more their mirror neurons – which are designed to read and copy what they see – will pick up and emulate restraint. The benefit to you is that because of the

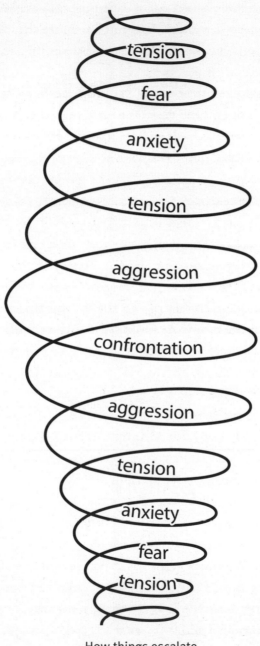

How things escalate

neuroplasticity of your own brain, the more you can practise being calm the more the brain reactivity pathways actually change. Simply put:

» **Restrained reactions** activate and create **calm pathways** for the future, while
» **Combustive reactions** result in **ever escalating confrontational patterns** of response.

This is how learning to breathe properly actually helps to calm the system:

» When your amygdala detects threat, the chemical messengers tell the body to get ready to run. This is characterised by panting and panic breathing.
» However, breathing deeply from your diaphragm sends a message via the vagus nerve that panic is over and the body/mind can resume normal function.
» For diaphragm breathing, a good trick is to imagine your ribs are a balloon:

1. As you breathe in, allow your ribcage to expand as your lungs fill with oxygen and inflate the balloon.
2. It is the exhalation that is key and plays a significant part in training your brain to tolerate (and thereby reduce) anxiety.
3. When you breathe out, exhale as much air as you can. Stretch your hands to relax clenched fists and drop your shoulders, rather like a sigh. You will feel calmer and better equipped to tackle the job in hand in a matter of minutes.

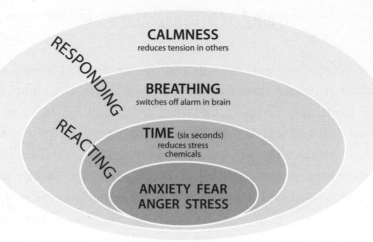

CALMNESS
reduces tension in others

BREATHING
switches off alarm in brain

TIME (six seconds)
reduces stress
chemicals

ANXIETY FEAR
ANGER STRESS

RESPONDING

REACTING

Reactions and responses

DE-STRESSING ACTIVITIES

At the earliest sign of ongoing anxiety take **preventative action** with simple coping, calming and relaxing strategies. Think about what you find relaxing and enjoyable so that you can reach for it when the anxiety begins to mount. For instance running, listening to music, watching a film, talking to a friend or grabbing a hug.

These help raise the levels of **good biochemicals** in your system – oxytocin, endorphins, dopamine, serotonin, vasopressin to name a few (see Chapter 2). Self-induced positive experiences will reduce your heightened toxic stress hormones, cortisol and adrenalin, and calm your inner terrain. This will result in a **more relaxed home environment,** which teenagers instantly notice, absorb and reflect back in **calmer behaviour.**

CREATING A CONTAGIOUS ATMOSPHERE

How often have you been in a filthy mood at home only to have it replicated and offered back in spades by your children, resulting in mayhem all round? What is happening is what's called emotional contagion. This is where one person's emotional state permeates the whole group. As it is being absorbed and replicated from the primitive and subconscious areas of your brain, it is difficult to stop without being explicitly aware of it.

Teenagers are more reactive than adults and may therefore exert their own infectious, often negative, temperaments back into the family melting pot. Next time this happens, try keeping yourself out of the negative energy cycle. Getting dragged into their negative state is like throwing another log on the fire.

MIRROR, MIRROR ON THE WALL

Meeting teenagers' anger with **level headedness** (as opposed to anger) or their sadness with **empathy** (as opposed to pity) helps them to stabilise their own emotions. Remember the brain's mirror neurons we talked about earlier? These are housed in your teenager's brain and they will **mimic** your responses and **reflect** back what they see. Not only will this change the texture of your interaction, but this new pattern will also be reflected in new tracks or templates in your developing teenager's brain. What you are **role-modelling** is calmness and resilience (the ability to bounce back from bad feelings), which can then be copied and rehearsed by their untrained brain.

NON-VERBAL COMMUNICATION

Children and adults are more sensitive to non-verbal signals than anything else and, in their hyper-vigilant emotional state, teens are especially so.

YOURS

Think of facial expressions, voice tone, intonations, gestures, body language and the way you use your eyes as ways to soothe your teenager and give them the sort of love and nurturance they still need, but find it difficult to ask for.

Think what it's like when someone says something to you in a clipped, sarcastic tone or doesn't bother to look at you. What you take away is what their attitude says, rather than what their words are saying. What is important is that what you show and say is consistent with what you feel. A teenager's radar will instantly detect false jolliness, thinly veiled toleration, gritted

teeth and firmly crossed arms – and jump to its own, often misjudged, conclusions.

As a rule of thumb, worry less about the words you use and focus more on how you deliver those words. With mood and non-verbal signals comprising around 85 per cent of the communication between you and your teenager, it is worth making sure that:

Your words + your body language + the underlying meaning of what you are saying are all the same.

Although teenagers are very good at being sarcastic and patronising, they find these types of interactions very confusing to process and they tend to react with extreme irritation, even if what you had intended was to highlight an issue in a light-hearted way. The more you can be aware of their responses to your efforts at banter, the more clues you will have to their inner state and to what sort of communication they need from you.

THEIRS

Although they need sensitive handling by us, they have yet to develop the art of offering that back. In addition, your teenager, robbed of much face-to-face interaction through hours communicating with a characterless screen, is less fluent in the language of reading social cues, often misinterpreting what is meant by other people's non-verbal signals. Teenagers can benefit from building awareness of their own body language and voice tone and what messages they might be unwittingly communicating to others.

You can help them by gently but firmly raising a flag when, for instance, they might be hurtful and rude to you or their siblings when they are in fact just tired. Let them know that it is okay for them to be tired and flat, but it isn't okay to take this out on other people. This helps them along the road of learning the impact that their behaviour is having on others around them and encourages them to find better coping strategies for themselves. *We as parents can help to pave the way by modelling and communicating non-verbally in a clear, straightforward way.*

ROLE-MODELLING

Parental influence naturally diminishes as teenagers start to slowly turn their focus of attention away from the heart of the family to the wider world. They will inevitably be influenced by their peers, celebrities, the media and the internet as they gather information that helps them to develop their identity. *This means that we need to work a lot harder to carve out space in our teenager's life and to maintain influence and hold their attention.*

Boys need male role models as they begin to cut the metaphorical apron strings at around the age of 13 and scan their world for an eye-catching male to emulate. This is the moment to try and ensure that any important men in your son's life (father, stepfather, older brother, cousin, grandfather, uncle, teacher) are role-modelling attitudes and behaviour that accord with your own values and vision for your growing son. He will adapt, adopt and develop habits and patterns, and put down behaviour templates based on what he imbibes.

The same applies to girls, who will also be watching interactions between close family members and basing their own behaviour on this.

If you are uncomfortable about someone who influences or is close to your teenager, try and have a clear, unambiguous and un-loaded chat to your child. Pick a moment when things are calm and they appear receptive and ready to talk. This is not about being judgemental and criticising. See it as an opportunity to highlight what you admire in others.

YOUR ROLE AS A ROLE MODEL

An important, if difficult, task is to have a good look at your own way of dealing with difficult situations. Do you draw on a range of skills to suit the problem or do you tend to default to an all-purpose sledgehammer approach?

» Do you tackle challenging situations by reacting in a **calm way** or is it road rage?

» Do you roll your sleeves up to sort issues in a **constructive, solution-focused way**?

» Do you avoid or **face up** to anything emotional/ confrontational?

» Are you a people pleaser? Do you avoid upsetting those close to you or can you **calmly assert your view**?

Your teenager will have absorbed, under your guidance, attitudes and beliefs surrounding a wealth of issues. Perhaps they just don their tin hat when the going gets tough? If, on the other hand, some of their approaches are too robust, now is the time to voice your concerns in a thoughtful, conversational way, inviting them to move to a more balanced standpoint.

CHAPTER KEY POINTS

» Being aware of what you value and where you stand on important issues helps to build a secure, well-boundaried home.

» Knowing what sets you off and how you react as a result helps you manage your reactions better.

» Calm, clear, straightforward verbal and non-verbal communication reduces family tension.

» Having an adaptable attitude as your teenager grows up encourages their cooperation and respect.

» Letting go of the reins gives your teenager the opportunity to learn the skills to manage their own challenges.

» Understanding and managing your stress levels role-models to your teenager how to do this too.

CHAPTER 4

PERSONALITY AND CHARACTER

– GETTING WIRED UP FOR ADULTHOOD

If we treat people as they are, we make them worse.
If we treat people as they ought to be, we help them
become what they are capable of becoming.
Haim G. Ginott, *Teacher and Child*

We have looked at how, when prompted by an experience, the biochemicals released in our bodies have an effect on our thoughts and feelings, which then results in the behaviour that others see. As we said, broadly speaking, good experiences produce good chemicals and a settled behaviour system (see page 28). *Now let's have a look at the broad personality types that our teenager might be moving towards as a combined result of what they inherited (nature) and what they are experiencing (nurture), and what we can do to nudge those tendencies in a more desirable direction.*

THE NUTS AND BOLTS OF PERSONALITY

Personality is discernable by the sorts of behaviours to which a person tends to default. In our teenagers we begin to think of them as predictable because the child can normally be guaranteed to demonstrate particular behaviours when pushed in a certain way. The boy who goes off in a week-long sulk because he can't have what he wants will slowly start being considered to have a sulky personality; the girl who hits the roof and argues hard at the hint of a 'No' might be seen as rebellious or demanding.

But remember that we now know that behavioural ups and downs are not a conscious choice. Instead, they reflect your teenager's developing ability to process their emotional reactions in response to their moment-to-moment experiences. Their shifting emotions are the fuel that is stoking and building their personality template.

A lot of work has been done on the idea of personality . Our thinking is that because we will learn to react and respond in certain ways to things that frighten or panic us, a good starting point when thinking about personality is to look at those gut fight/flight/freeze reactions triggered in the primitive brain. Because teenage personality is still forming, we may find that our teens flit between reactions, but despite this there will normally be a predominant style to which they default when the pressure is on. As a mechanism for handling high-stress situations it is fine for them to be pushed into one of these styles if the going is really tough (an emergency, an exam, a performance, an argument with a friend). But if you find that tiny triggers (they forget their games kit, they have an earlier curfew than they'd hoped for, they lose a tennis match) are setting off a full-scale meltdown, that's the signal to try and influence some changes.

FIGHT, FLIGHT OR FREEZE REACTIONS

Let's look at these styles and how they might link into personality. Broadly:

» A **fight** reaction has a tendency to attack when under pressure.
» A **flight** reaction has a tendency to run and hide and avoids challenging situations.
» A **freeze** reaction has a tendency to being helpless (as if paralysed) when under pressure.

Every teenager will have different thresholds for assessing how threatening or anxiety-provoking an experience is for them. What sends one child into a frenzy of panic is easily taken in the stride of another. So what causes such diverse responses? Their genetic predisposition (emotionally robust versus overly sensitive) will of course play a part, as will memories that have been logged as a result of life and family experiences, as well as the way a child is starting to view the world – their positive or negative developing mindset. Where one teenager finds giving things a go an exciting and challenging prospect, another will find moving out of their comfort zone frightening to contemplate.

As your teenager's patterns of reactions and responses become embedded they steadily evolve into the predictable habits you watch them adopt when things go wrong or when they are up against it. These are becoming behavioural pathways as the brain is growing and developing and their personality starts to emerge out of these default behaviours. Each of us during our lifetime forms habitual responses to certain experiences/situations/people and when faced with something similar, a chain of unconscious biological body/mind processes will be triggered.

PERSONALITY AS A PROCESS

Bear in mind that our personalities are not static. They are a fluid process that is the culmination of how our thoughts, feelings and behaviours connect and affect each other in a constantly moving course. Our responses to experiences trigger how our feelings and thoughts work together, resulting in the behaviour that is visible to others. *This is why watching our children closely is such a key part of knowing what we need to do to help them manage things better.* Observing their behaviour gives clues to their personality, character and temperament, but what is visible is only part of the picture.

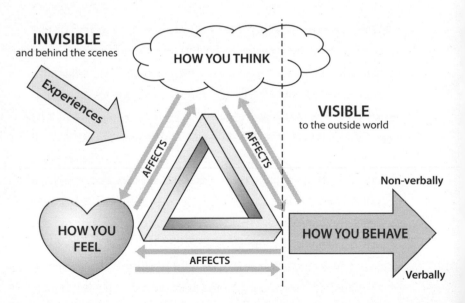

Personality as a process

A day-to-day experience (for example, being ignored by a friend) is picked up by the teen radar (the amygdala that we referred to earlier), which then pushes their reactor button releasing a cocktail of stress chemicals into their system. They feel hurt, sad or lonely and their thoughts start taking a negative turn ('This always happens to me', 'Nobody likes me') and these things together start stoking the behaviour engine. The behaviour we see will be influenced by whether their reaction tendency is fight, flight or freeze. A child prone towards fight may respond by lashing out at a sibling, someone who tends towards flight might slope off to their bedroom, while a freeze style is likely to fall into a black hole of helplessness.

SKILLS AND ABILITIES FOR AN EVEN TEMPERAMENT

For some teenagers, their thoughts and feelings will remain reasonably steady as different experiences hit them. Others will be impacted much more acutely. We have listed below some of the skills or abilities that make for a more even temperament. Children who have high levels of these abilities are able to mobilise them even under stress, so that they cope well with events and remain more easily in their settled systems.

Being able to:

» Have a clear sense of the world.
» Recognise and express inner emotions.
» Cooperate and listen to the opinions of others.
» Weigh up different choices and make balanced decisions.
» Communicate in a clear, straightforward way.
» Delay gratification by waiting, observing and reflecting before reacting.

HELPING THEM FIND EMOTIONAL STABILITY

Children who have not learnt to process their emotional responses to difficult situations in healthy functional ways are more likely to develop difficult behaviour patterns. The extreme end of this spectrum would be to develop negative strategies in order to cope with situations. We look at these negative coping strategies, such as eating disorders, self-harming and addiction, in detail in Chapters 6 and 7.

WHAT DOES BEHAVIOUR ACHIEVE?

All behaviour is communicating an underlying emotional need and that need is for your attention.[1] Your small child developed certain strategies to get that much-needed attention from you, even if it was negative. Very quickly they worked out that complaining, sulking, tantrums, being overly shy, playing the buffoon or turning on the charm got rapid results, so your child turned to these readily when your attention was waning. Slowly, a trademark pattern of behaviour became established.

With the plasticity in the teenage brain, we now have another chance to influence these patterns. The way we as parents respond and react, for example to the hissy fit or the strop, can either reinforce or diminish that default pattern and this is where our role comes in. If we can use our empathy to try and see our child's unsettled (or unacceptable and annoying) behaviours as being grounded in feelings of panic, fear and rage, this will help moderate our irritation. It will also help us to remind ourselves that reacting to these patterns is like giving the child's behaviour muscle a good workout.

Encouraging positive behaviour, on the other hand, is a slow process. Learning any new skill requires patience and encouragement, as well as practice and reinforcement in order to develop fluency.

INVESTIGATIVE PARENTING

Before you as a parent can take proactive steps to establish positive personality traits and behaviours, it is helpful to take some time to really watch your teenager and build an awareness of their unique behavioural style.

The first step is to identify what is going on with your child based on what you sense, see and hear. Unsettled and fluctuating ups and downs of feelings, thoughts, attitudes and behaviours are normal, provided they are not dominant. *Because our emotional states can be felt by those around us, take time to tune into your child and use your intuition about where you think they are emotionally in order to guide the changes you want to encourage.*

Have a look at the settled and unsettled feelings and thought processes below to give you a better sense of where your teenager might be emotionally.

SETTLED AND UNSETTLED FEELINGS AND THOUGHT PROCESSES

Settled feelings	Unsettled feelings
Even keel	Overreacts, volatile, drama queen
Resilient – gets back on track	Needs cheering up or bolstering
Humble – able to ask for help	Proud, arrogant
Empowered – feels able to influence events	Powerless – feels at the mercy of events

Settled feelings	Unsettled feelings
Tolerant	Intolerant
Motivated	Apathetic – can't be bothered
Energetic	Lethargic
Exercises self-control	Lacks self-control
Enthusiastic	Bored
Vulnerable	Victim
Empathic	Me, me, me – selfish
Trusting	Suspicious
Self-assured	Uncertain
Safe and secure	Frightened
Has fun and relaxes	Worried, anxious, can't let go and enjoy
Cares about others	Cares predominantly about self

Settled thought processes	Unsettled thought processes
Objective, rational	Subjective, me focused
Clear, focused	Confused, uncertain
Resolves fallouts – rupture/repair	Falls out – rupture/despair
Optimistic	Pessimistic
Realistic	Fantasy world, unrealistic outlook
Gives things a go	Reticent
Curious	Uninterested
Reflects, then responds	Knee-jerk reactions
Okay to make mistakes	Failure = shame and humiliation

Settled thought processes	Unsettled thought processes
Says no (when necessary)	Agrees, follows, sulks
Takes losses on the chin	Competitive (and aggressive)
Balances strengths/weaknesses	Self-deprecatory/boasts
Reasonable	Unreasonable
Accountable – accepts blame	Not my fault
Aware of self and others	Unaware of impact of self on others
Accepts boundaries	Pushes and pushes to get own way
Respects limits	Loses temper, sullen, disobeys, revengeful
I can, I will, I'll try	I can't, I won't, don't make me
Respects individuality and difference	Criticises, complains, judges others
Accepts pecking order	Sharp elbows, must be best
Assumes responsibility	Irresponsible, relies on/follows others
Lets things go	Resents, harbours grudges

IDENTIFYING UNSETTLED PERSONALITY TYPES

Whenever you see signs of the thoughts and feelings outlined above that are associated with unsettled behaviour, you can be fairly sure that anxiety is at the root. In physiological terms, it is accompanied by the release of adrenalin into the system when a situation is read by the body as a threat to survival. It will result in a sense of being on red alert. If the anxiety switch remains locked on it will affect physical and mental good health as the body and brain remain on guard. High levels of anxiety play a significant part in undermining the ability to maintain healthy, happy relationships.

The work of the eminent psychologist and psychiatrist John Bowlby has been pivotal in elaborating on the origins of anxiety. His research showed that anxiety originates in early psychological development when 'separation anxiety' – the fear of loss or separation from the parent – felt paramount to the baby because survival depended on having the parent at hand to meet needs.[2] During the teenage years that anxiety resurfaces in a different form and we look at this in more detail in Chapter 8 (see pages 162–5). *Learning to increasingly tolerate this anxiety and manage life's problems on their own is a key skill for your teenager to develop.* During this teenage period, as the demands on them intensify, certain behavioural patterns can start to take root as mechanisms to manage anxiety.

IMPLEMENTING CHANGE – PERSONALITY STYLES AND EFFECTIVE PARENT RESPONSES

Once you have noticed some patterns and identified repeating behaviours which, when the chips are down, have a tendency to rear their ugly heads, you have a chance to make some changes to the way you respond to your child when their unsettled behaviour button has been pressed. A red flag for you is when things are heading downhill and you become aware that certain behaviours are becoming a regular pattern and you are gloomily thinking, 'Here we go, this old chestnut again…'

However, possibly the biggest obstacle to change is parental expectations. Try and keep these reasonable. Changes in behaviour require not only your attention, but also quantities of patience. If a behaviour has been going on for a while it is unlikely to change overnight. Attempting to change behaviour

is like using a dimmer switch – you start with modest changes, but as long as you've started the process and you keep going you will get there in the end.

We have listed below some exaggerated generic personality styles grouped into the three fight/flight/freeze categories. This will help you identify what you may need to focus on with regard to your responses. The long-term goal here is to help your child deal with their own challenges confidently and independently without resorting to stressful outbursts, passive helplessness or the negative strategies covered in Chapters 6 and 7. Learning to do this will boost their self-esteem and confidence, and bolster their resilience.

PERSONALITY STYLES

Think back to the fight/flight/freeze responses earlier in this chapter. Because unsettled behaviours will cluster around these categories, it is useful to start recognising any specific traits in your child.

Fight personalities have a tendency to unpredictability. They may ignite quickly when provoked, resulting in confrontation, disrespect or being a drama queen. They may also be selfish or uncooperative, but also competitive, with high expectations of themselves and others.

Flight personalities may have a tendency to be oversensitive, preferring to withdraw in conflict or discussion, and may come across as moody or negative. They will tend to brush things under the carpet and pretend they are fine by acting shy or jokey.

Freeze personalities have a tendency to paralysis, lethargy and helplessness when under stress. They can be worriers and will tend to comply with others' wishes in order to gain reassuring approval.

Here are some behavioural tendencies that link to the three stress responses and give us a clue about the feelings lurking underneath. We have included a few suggested parent responses in each case to give you a sense of what works in managing that particular tendency. You'll find more on parent responses in Chapter 8.

Fight Behaviours

1. Confrontational/no boundaries
2. Disrespectful/rude
3. Demanding/competitive/driven/selfish
4. Rebellious/uncooperative
5. Drama queen/flappy

1. Confrontational/no boundaries

Teenager: 'I am used to getting what I want and, if you want me to resort to one of my 57 varieties of strategies in order to achieve what I want, then I will. If someone plays the "no" game with me, I might throw all my toys out of the pram or get really down. People hate seeing me upset so they give in, and that makes me nice again. Victory and power only give me a brief, short-lived high, so I have to keep pressing on for bigger, better, faster and higher.'

Helpful parent responses:

» Impose boundaries and limits in a consistent and clear way.
» Help them to develop a sense of responsibility.
» They have to learn how to tolerate disappointment by not always getting their own way.
» Link actions to consequences so that they understand their behaviour has an impact on other people too.

2. Disrespectful/rude

Teenager: 'I like everything to be just perfect and I get angry when things are not just so. Apparently I fly off the handle easily and get rude and insolent when people touch my stuff or I lose a game or things don't go my way, but that's just not true. I expect to be number one and demand it of myself. What's wrong with that?'

Helpful parent responses:

» Rudeness is a case of overreacting due to being unable to manage feelings. Respond to this with calm firmness and try and address the expectations underneath.

» Check out goal-setting and help the child to be easier on themselves by helping them moderate perfectionist ideas about their ability, looks, achievements and aspirations. These high expectations stoke the anger engine because it is always primed for disappointment, frustration or turning to blame someone else when things have not turned out perfectly.

3. Demanding/competitive/driven/selfish

Teenager: 'I live for praise and prizes, so if I can win trophies and be top dog, then I get the attention I need. I can keep focused and drive myself endlessly to achieve what I want – sometimes that might be to do well in something but it might also be to get my own way. I love being in the centre with the world revolving around me, me, me.'

Helpful parent responses:
» Applaud the child's effort and participation rather than only acknowledging their achievements.
» Recognise some of their ways of being, rather than simply what they achieve (e.g. 'I really appreciated your help yesterday' or 'You were really kind and patient with your sister').
» Respond positively to realistic and reasonable requests but don't be afraid to say no too. This teaches the child to distinguish between what is reasonable and not.
» Encourage them to recognise and applaud the achievements of others, for example their siblings.

4. Rebellious/uncooperative

Teenager: 'I am really confused about this business of rules, limits, laws. And what is compliance? Being part of a team? I just don't think I should have to fall in line if I don't feel like it. If I don't want to do something, it is a free world and I should be entitled to do as I please!'

Helpful parent responses:
- » Set up opportunities for the child to do things for you in order that you can demonstrate your approval, love and gratitude in very small ways. A quiet thank you, a wink or a genuine act of appreciation will teach them the benefit of working with people, rather than always being in opposition.
- » Avoid bribes or enforced compliance – you are trying to ignite their intrinsic wish to cooperate, which in turn makes their relationship with you feel secure.
- » Use minimal sarcasm/cynicism/criticism as this will trigger further rebellion.

5. Drama queen/flappy

Teenager: 'I always seem to be going from one drama to another and it's quite draining. The smallest misunderstanding can trip my switch and then I am liable to detonate. I am used to lurching from crisis to crisis, and because I have a reputation for award-winning histrionic solo performances, they tend to gather a participatory audience.'

Helpful parent responses:
- » Try to remain calmly anchored and not get hooked into reacting and responding to their drama.

» Help them to help themselves by modelling level-headed, rational and considerate behaviour.

» When things have calmed down try and talk them through the impact this episode has had on you, without resorting to judgement or criticism.

Flight Behaviours
1. Victim/negative
2. Overly sensitive/reactive
3. Avoiding/not communicating

1. Victim/negative

Teenager: 'I am a cup half-empty person. Everything always goes wrong for me. I never get it right. I should be better than I am but I feel powerless to do anything to change things. I am stuck hovering between feelings of panic, fear and anger and I feel much better when someone takes charge and tells me what I need to do.'

Helpful parent responses:
» These tendencies are to do with patterns of thinking so try challenging 'Things always go wrong' by reminding them of times when things went right, e.g. 'What about when...?'

» Flag up and attend to any positives (events, character-istics, memories, times spent together) before they try and gain your attention by offering a negative observation.

» Offer practical opportunities to help them overcome their fear of getting things wrong, e.g. encourage them to make some of their own arrangements such as booking their own train tickets. Resist the temptation to swoop in, rescue and do it for them.

» Help them bounce back when things go wrong as their low resilience is often responsible for their passive state. Applaud their efforts when they do make their own decisions, however small.

2. Overly sensitive/reactive

Teenager: 'The smallest thing trips my switch and then people hurt or upset me and I can't bear that as I find it really hard to contain my feelings. I am quite fragile and protected by eggshells so that people tread very carefully around me. I am always worried that something will go wrong and I often find it hard to gauge how others are feeling.'

Helpful parent responses:
» Gently help the child become aware of their own overreactions (but not in the heat of the moment) and suggest how they can start responding in a more appropriate way.
» Demonstrate a range of reactions yourself so they can begin to see that different levels of trigger (mislaying your keys versus crashing the car) should produce different degrees of distress.
» Encourage them to express what they are feeling so that they can begin to manage their emotional world better.

3. Avoiding/not communicating

Teenager: 'I don't really like talking to people about my troubles and I'd much rather disappear off to my room, especially if adults start asking me about things. I can spend hours dreaming up mad plans. Sometimes I get very despondent and ruminate about things so they grow out of proportion. I can slip into low moods quite easily but I prefer not to ask for help.'

Helpful parent responses:
>   » Allow space and privacy but also make sure that they interact with everyone else as much as possible.
>   » Limit time allowed for solo tasks, like gaming, which further compound isolation and low mood.
>   » Encourage them to talk by opening conversations about non-personal topics. Slowly build on this as they become better able to express and articulate themselves.
>   » Be careful of not being judgemental or opinionated in your conversations as they will shut down for fear of being judged themselves.

Freeze Behaviours
1. Worried/anxious/lonely
2. Overly compliant/shy
3. Lethargic/tired all the time
4. Sulking

1. Worried/anxious/lonely
Teenager: 'I feel quite isolated and find it hard to reach out for help with my worries, which swim around in my head. I'm terrified of doing the wrong thing and ending up with a big problem so I find it easier to do nothing. I sometimes feel paralysed – as though I just can't work out what to do. People get exasperated with me but I'm afraid to give things a go and I'm good at putting up a cheerful façade.'

Helpful parent responses:

» Try and acknowledge how the child feels by helping them to talk about their feelings and being there as a safety net.

» Irritating as their behaviour can be, try not to show this as it will inflame the anxiety and fear.

» Make them aware of some of your own mistakes so they begin to see that getting things wrong sometimes is okay.

» Encourage participation in activities so that they can build self-confidence.

2. Overly compliant/shy

Teenager: 'When I was little everyone looked at me and fussed over me. That shut me up. Mum always let me hide in her skirt and that felt safe when everyone stared at me. I didn't often talk but once I did and the whole room looked at me, which was excruciatingly embarrassing, so I won't do that again! I'd much rather just do what people want and keep my head below the parapet so I don't get noticed.'

Helpful parent responses:

» Present small opportunities for the child to take centre stage, e.g. family mealtimes.

» Encourage them to assert themselves and fight their own battles; if this child stands their ground occasionally (e.g. with a sibling), respect their autonomy.

» Avoid focusing on and giving attention to the shyness.

» Slowly try and build awareness of how their behaviour may be alienating them from others.

3. Lethargic/tired all the time

Teenager: 'I reckon it is better to have not tried, than to have tried, failed and suffered the shame and humiliation of everyone knowing that I didn't manage it. At least this way it looks as though I couldn't care less and it's so much easier to just do what comes easily than to work hard at something.'

Helpful parent responses:

- » Don't confuse lethargic with lazy. Use your intuition to work out whether it is fear or carelessness.
- » Encourage activities/situations that are guaranteed to give the feel-good factor, raise spirits and put optimistic fuel back in the tank.
- » Break down goals into small bite-sized tasks and try and kick-start the child's motivation for each of these.
- » Drip-feed appropriate levels of praise and encouragement (no pushing).

4. Sulking

Teenager: 'I can't articulate what I am feeling or what I want and I can't bear to get into any form of confrontation. Sometimes I can brood and ponder over small issues for days and then they get inflated and grow out of proportion in my head. It feels as though people keep doing things to me. I find it really difficult to say how I feel and that makes me feel angry and resentful.'

Helpful parent responses:

- » Resist getting hooked into reacting to this behaviour by attending to the sulking in any way, for example by teasing, sarcasm or pandering.
- » Encourage the child by asking questions in a clear,

unloaded way to teach them how to articulate their needs: 'Are you okay? You seem unhappy. Can I help? Try and tell me what is wrong and that will help me to understand.'

» Whenever possible, respond to their needs when they are clearly articulated.

» Help the child to see that it is impossible for others to second-guess their problems.

Underneath this iceberg of unsettled behaviours is a cauldron of unsettled thoughts and feelings bubbling away. Being aware of the possible invisible causes and aiming to respond to them, as well as to the visible behaviour, is the most effective way of managing, and even improving, these developing personality traits. Have a look at the feelings wheel on page 40 to remind yourself of the core feelings that might underlie behaviours.

CHAPTER KEY POINTS

» A character develops as a result of a distinctive pattern of responses, reactions and interactions that become observable by other people as behaviour.

» As personality styles emerge during the teenage years, these behavioural habits get hardwired into the brain ready for adulthood.

» You have a window of opportunity to recognise certain characteristics and traits in your teenager during their brain renovations and have a hand in fine-tuning them.

» Your responses to certain behaviours either strengthen or weaken them.

CHAPTER 5

TEENAGE BEHAVIOURS, HABITS AND PASTIMES
– WHAT IS NORMAL AND WHEN SHOULD I BE CONCERNED?

*[Teenagers are] looking for something to struggle against
… At the very least it gives teenagers something to complain
about.So if the parents keep giving in, the teenager has to
embark on a desperate search for some behaviour that will get
a reaction, and the conflict will be escalated until the parents
do make a stand, or the children burn the house down.*
John Cleese and Robin Skynner,
Families and How to Survive Them

'Why on earth do they do what they do?' This has been the
exasperated cry from generations of parents. Recent discoveries
about brain changes can help us piece together a clearer picture,
which explains why it is inevitable that the teenage years will
be a period of emotional flux, behavioural change, uncertainty

and challenge. *The focus of this chapter is on understanding what drives teenagers to normal experimentation and how this can sometimes develop into something more troubling.*

Society is focused heavily on the problems associated with teenagers, be it the rising levels of teenage depression, aggression, addiction or unsociable behaviour. There seems to be a perpetual witch-hunt for who can be blamed for the malaise:

» Is it the fault of the parent? **or**
» Should we point the finger of blame at the government or schools? **or**
» The media and the internet? **or**
» The companies producing cheap alcohol, pills to pop, fast food or cigarettes?

Focusing on dramas and whose fault it is serves only to achieve ever more heightened levels of anxiety and stress. This headless-chicken approach leads everyone involved to avoid taking responsibility for deepening their understanding and exploring solutions for their own teenager. This means we end up aiming our firepower in the wrong direction.

We encourage you as parents to take a closer look at troubling teenage habits in Chapters 6 and 7 and to link your child's vulnerabilities (e.g. anxiety or anger) to the weak areas in their personalities (e.g. sulking or confrontational – see Chapter 4). *This helps to see the pastime (e.g. bowing to peer pressure, using social media or alcohol) for what it actually is: a coping strategy.* When under fire from all sides, as teenagers effectively are, it is the weak spot – their Achilles heel – that gives way.

This chapter is going to focus on the pathways towards dependency and addiction, in order that we gain a better understanding of why some teenagers end up in trouble while others don't. We will help you to assess the lie of the land both for yourself and your teenager so that you can fine-tune your interactions. There are early-warning behavioural tendencies long before a habit becomes a full-blown problem. *In order to understand what is going on we need to have a close look behind the scenes at the brain's reward centre and dopamine because they are both the problem and the solution.*

FINE-TUNING AND BALANCING THE TEENAGE BRAIN

The teenage brain is dependent on one vital ingredient above all others in order to undertake the neural overhaul during adolescence, paving the way for a top-of-the-range adult brain. *That ingredient is dopamine, billed as the 'wonder drug'* (see page 31). Because teenagers are experiencing so many new things, they need the dopamine neurotransmitter to fire up connections between the brain's neurons, which enables learning. As a result teenagers appear to be biologically programmed to seek out the wonder drug through good sources, or indeed bad sources and activities (see Chapters 6 and 7).

If your teenager has a tendency to be easily stressed or is facing more problems or challenges than usual, they may have a greater need to rebalance their yo-yoing chemicals. If, on the other hand, their life experiences or inherent personality enables them to remain on a reasonably even keel, they are less at risk. However, all teenagers are vulnerable to some extent and the thing to watch for is if you are seeing a lot of their hallmark anxious behaviours. Trying to get themselves on an even keel is what is likely to lead them down what we call temptation

alley (the wrong crowd, alcohol, drugs, cigarettes, sex, gaming, gambling, pornography) in an effort to re-establish chemical and emotional equilibrium.

THE REWARD CENTRE – FIRED BY BIG PLEASURABLE PAY-OFFS

Let's have a closer look at this biological drive. It comes from the brain's reward centre (the RC) housed deep in the primitive and subconcious areas of the brain. *This means that it is an innate process and operates out of awareness rather than something rational or thought through.* When your teenager experiments with novel, risky or exciting experiences, it is the RC that is stirred into action and becomes flooded with feel-good dopamine. Experiences like food, sex, earning money, winning and succeeding all result in the RC firing on all cylinders, leaving the teenage brain motivated and alert. However, the shadow side is that the RC gets fired up by high-risk activities too, like gambling, alcohol and drugs (see Chapters 6 and 7).

MULTITALENTED DOPAMINE

An important piece of the jigsaw is that the RC in the brain is intrinsically kick-started by rewarding and pleasurable activities, but is fuelled by dopamine. Dopamine provides your teenager's get-up-and-go and the good feeling that is responsible for topping up their levels of motivation and enthusiasm. Their biological drive will be automatically scanning their environment for experiences that fire this system. *Put simply, the biological imperative will ensure that dopamine is activated either through positive pastimes or via temptation alley.*

Dopamine is the key player in establishing settled and cooperative behaviour. Good levels help teenagers to do more of the following:

Be Curious and Alert

Back in the days when we were cave people the brain relied on its highly tuned sense of smell, which guided cave people's innate drive to seek things out, survive, explore and learn, resulting in triumphant feelings when efforts were rewarded with dopamine. (This was in the days before the cortex (Brain 3) arrived with all its sophisticated strategising, rational thinking and planning.) It still works like this today and this is what drives your teenager to seek out and explore the wider world in preparation for independence.

Behave Well

Humans are the only mammals who have developed the capacity to push fear, anger or hurt under the carpet. If we are sad we can cheer ourselves up by seeking out a particular person or distracting ourselves with an activity, which will boost dopamine supplies. Other animals cannot do this. Their feelings are more transparent and these are translated into knee-jerk behavioural responses that are painfully evident (the cowering dog or the bolting horse). For humans, Brain 3 has the ability to learn how to override gut feelings, control impulses and think rationally. These are all brain activities that assist in directing us to good settled behaviour. However, when it comes to our teenager we need to remind ourselves that due to reconstruction work in Brain 3, exercising restraint and sound judgement is much harder.

Feel Motivated

Teenagers' get-up-and-go, energy, motivation, enthusiasm and ability to learn is switched on by curiosity, interest and pleasure in exciting, novel or risky experiences and is powered by dopamine. Your teenager needs to be in this dopamine zone in order to focus, pay attention and enjoy learning at school. Boredom, lack of interest and hating a subject or a teacher are sure signs of low dopamine.

Be Cooperative

Not only does feel-good dopamine come from doing things, it also comes from having good close relationships, for instance with you their parent. As babies, they were programmed to bond with you and to please you, as this was vital to survival. Their closeness to you continued to give them their dopamine hit through their younger years. But as they move towards adolescence, this becomes trickier because they need to feel independent from you, but also need to cooperate with you to trigger their dopamine. Good collaborative interactions with you at home will develop into a blueprint that will roll out in their other close relationships.

FEEL-GOOD HIGH

We need to remember that high-grade peak performance dopamine also comes from any physical activity and experience that involves action and energy. However, low-grade dopamine is produced, but also quickly depleted, by stimulating sedentary activities like watching TV, gaming, gambling, pornography, drinking sessions and certain drugs (more on this in Chapters 6 and 7). These activities generate a very intense and short-term feel-good factor, but the long-term reward for using them for self-regulation is dependency and addiction.

BLAME THOSE KILLJOY PARENTS!

It is worth noting here that a parent's stance can have a negative impact on teenage behaviour. There's more on fine-tuning parent responses with your teenager in Chapter 8, but in the meantime be wary of the following:

» We (as parents) are a guaranteed button pusher while our child is trying to put more psychological distance between themselves and us, so our very presence is sometimes incendiary. Try not to drive your teenager to be more rebellious through the way you say things to them.
» In this highly sensitive stage, teenagers can easily catapult into their unsettled (irritated/scared/confused/angry) cortisol-ridden state, which in turn zaps vital dopamine supplies, intensifying their stress and irritation.

» As parents, we should be a vital source of reassurance but when the tap is turned off (perhaps as a result of your teenager's unacceptable behaviour) this can result in an emotional meltdown.

» Parents can also be a fun sponge, killing their teenager's hedonistic joyride with their get-back-to-the-real-world deflating logic.

» Parents can be a source of constant disapproval so that the child becomes oversensitive to the slightest hint of criticism. This will provoke either rebellion or an unnatural need to comply.

GETTING THE RIGHT HABITS ESTABLISHED

If we are really lucky, our teenager is getting their **feel-good dopamine supply** from **desirable experiences** such as playing rugby or netball, investigating the laws of relativity, reading Shakespeare, tidying their room, doing Pilates, helping unquestioningly with household chores or playing with friends before turning in for an early night. However, few parents will be housing teenagers who are conforming quite so obligingly... If they are, their child will be experiencing a **perfect balance of feel-good chemicals, their RC will be primed and firing** and their **behaviour will be exemplary.**

HOW COME TEENAGERS VARY SO MUCH?

We are now going to look at why teenagers can be so different from one another. Experimentation – good and bad – is normal and to be expected as they are growing up. But we need to know why some teenagers will head off down the slippery slope to addictive behaviour while others can experiment safely and stay on track. This can be a time of mounting frustration for us because many of their choices and activities lack foresight or hindsight and they end up in trouble. *To us it may appear like stupidity, but perhaps it makes more sense when we remember that rational Brain 3, engaged with its overhaul, is not calling the shots.*

EMOTIONAL SENSITIVITY

Today's world is heavily weighed towards external pressures, which are providing the predominant experience for teenagers. However, for some, these external pressures may be playing havoc with their ability to regulate their levels of stress chemicals. Pressure comes in the guise of:

- » Academic achievement, competition/challenge, sporting success, fear of failure.
- » High potential for disappointment/unrealistic goals, pushy parents, overly controlling/highly inflated expectations.
- » Materialism/must-have gadgets, media/fashion/airbrushed perfection.
- » Pornography/sex gods and goddesses, fantasy beliefs about relationships/performance.
- » Social media/unrealistic ideals of universal popularity and anxiety concerning social inclusion.

» Peer pressure – 'Everyone else is doing it so why can't I?'
» Uncertainty over future/body image/identity/career.
» Home life with confusing boundaries/punishments, varying levels of security/insecurity among blended families.
» Parents stressed/divorced/preoccupied with financial and midlife problems.

An emotional litmus test measuring the body's biochemistry among today's teenagers might show high cortisol/low dopamine in stressed teenagers, versus high dopamine/low cortisol levels in self-assured ones.

EMOTIONAL TOLERANCE

Different life experiences or personal history will result in varying degrees of unsettled feelings and behaviours and therefore different tolerance thresholds.

Change is something that can upset the teenage apple cart very easily, for instance: attending a new school/leaving school, facing new challenges/the future, gaining new friends, developing a new identity, growing up, divorce, house moves, births/deaths. This is not to suggest that when a child encounters any of these experiences they will definitely reach for the more extreme coping strategies outlined in Chapter 6, such as self-harm or eating disorders, in order to ride the storm. But what is clear is that they will potentially be more vulnerable.

RESILIENCE VARIATIONS

Even the most grounded teenager will find that when the pressures become too intense they will scan round for activities to help them cope and feel better. These activities are what we mean by coping strategies. They may be healthy ones like taking some exercise, listening to music or relaxing with friends (more on these later in this chapter). Or they may be unhealthy coping strategies like popping pills, controlling eating habits or binge drinking.

Remember that the motivation to subliminally seek out an external coping strategy is in order to rebalance inner biochemicals, so look out for evidence of emotional turmoil that will alert you to their inner needs. So for instance, for us as parents a glass of wine works after a busy, stressful day, as does a bar of chocolate, a run or a cuddle. Like adults, children will vary in their need for coping strategies in terms of the ones they reach for and in their susceptibility to the more negative ones, so attune yourself to their preferences. For example a nervous, introverted teenage girl is unlikely to vent her anxiety by going on a pub crawl with the lads, getting arrested by the police and spending the night sobering up in a cell. Her way of coping is more likely to be more inward and private. Equally, a fit rugby-playing teenage boy is unlikely to numb his emotional pain with secretive self-harming behaviour like cutting. His strategies are more likely to turn outwards.

HORMONAL CHAOS

Think of the hormonal roller coaster that is going on in teenagers as they hit puberty. The hormones oestrogen and testosterone are the key players and their rise plays a huge role in destabilising emotional equilibrium. For girls, oestrogen boosts dopamine and oxytocin production, which is welcome, but its fluctuations also depress serotonin levels, so you may notice your daughter becoming moodier. There is similar upheaval in the male camp. Serotonin, which inhibits aggressive behaviour, is naturally lower in adolescent boys. Added to this, mounting testosterone levels also conspire to promote a more aggressive attitude in boys, but more lethargy as well, and more interest in sex and higher risk taking. Testosterone also inhibits the ability to talk and socialise, resulting in the grunting that many of us face from our sons.

IT'S NOT JUST THEIR DNA!

Different children, even from the same DNA pool, will have a wide variance in their genetic predisposition, resulting in varying levels of:

- » Anxiety toleration (stress/panic tipping point)
- » Emotional robustness (sensitivity)
- » Resilience (bouncing back)
- » Hormones (mood ups and downs)
- » Dopamine levels (optimistic enthusiasm/feeling good)
- » Focus and learning (attention discrepancy)
- » Need for comfort/reassurance (attention seeking)
- » Addiction tendency (dependency)

Thinking about your own child in the context of these factors listed above gives you vital clues.

In terms of actual DNA, it is now widely accepted that 50 per cent of a child's vulnerability towards an addictive behaviour is genetic and the rest is down to circumstances, peer group and media pressure. Whatever the nature/nurture balance, each child will develop their own cruise control setting while experimenting with life's bigger playing field, taking risks or seeking pleasure.

EXPERIMENTATION AND RISK – MOVING CONFIDENTLY OUT OF THE COMFORT ZONE

So what is going to make teenagers get this risk/safety/reward balance right? In the first instance, teenagers need to feel good and confident and encouraged to take those first steps into the wider world. Different, novel experiences offer them the potential for healthy experimentation, for example more time away from home, new friends, bigger schools, travel, sex, driving, university or a new job. When they accomplish these successfully, this will result in their body producing rewarding dopamine. This in turn will leave them feeling good about themselves and their ability and confidence to try more things out.

However, they are also likely to dabble in a range of other new activities like staying up all night, alcohol or cigarettes. They may discover that some of these activities miraculously make them feel good/numbed and, by chance, enable them to cope with underlying emotional turbulence like social anxiety or pressure.

DRIVING WITHOUT DUE CARE AND ATTENTION

The drive for **experimentation and risk** for some teenagers may be likened to driving a car with an overzealous accelerator and a gravely inadequate braking system. **Dopamine** (and testosterone) act like high-spirited accelerators, while **serotonin,** which acts as the brain's chemical brake, struggles to do its job as levels fall during puberty (see Chapter 2).

The more your teenager is easily overwhelmed and finds themselves getting stuck in an unsettled emotional state, unable to find a way to get back on track, the more vulnerable they are to needing to restore inner calm by turning to these negative activities and strategies.

DE-STRESSING HABITS AND HEALTHY COPING STRATEGIES

The journey through adolescence is rarely plain sailing and teenagers need to develop healthy ways of coping with difficult periods. By now you may not be surprised to realise that the most prevalent underlying emotional state that teenagers report is fear and anxiety about life and their future. They may appear to be fine, but this often masks varying levels of frantic paddling under the surface. It is vital that, alongside this pandemonium, they also get the opportunity to develop a set of healthy coping strategies, which can in time become the habits of choice to be called upon when the going gets really tough.

There are lots of activities that help introduce and balance biochemicals in the system by reducing stress levels, positively boosting feelings, restoring calm when life feels uncertain and ensuring future well-being. Any healthy activity that makes you feel better able to cope with life works because it:

» Raises feelings of optimism and suppresses stress, thereby realigning emotional equilibrium.
» Programmes itself into the reward 'I'll have more of that' system, making it a spontaneous habit.
» Reinforces that positive activity as the habit of choice for the future.

Help your child to become aware of healthy ways to alleviate their stress and cope with pressure and its emotional effects.

Knowing what works for them and when to reach for a strategy will help them produce the feel-good chemicals they need to keep their mental and emotional state balanced. This will boost energy and motivation and keep your teenager in their settled behaviour system where they will be calmer, less anxious, frightened or angry and more resilient in tolerating life's ups and downs. You can help to pave the way by discussing the healthy ways in which you cope with your own stress and making sure you are 'walking the talk' by using some of these strategies yourself.

» Seeking **help** and receiving it provides valuable advice and relief from problems.
» Mindfulness and meditation promote **relaxation** while alleviating anxiety through focusing on the present and regulating **breathing**.
» Being with **animals** provides comfort and an opportunity to be responsible and caring.
» Giving challenging activities a go promotes motivation and an **'I can' attitude**.
» **Creative** interests keep all areas of the brain active and offer distraction.
» Charity and **voluntary work** develop empathy and promotes feelings of fulfilment.
» **Socialising** develops bonds and connections outside the family.
» Having **conversations** helps to put problems in perspective and prevents emotions being bottled up.
» **Music** relaxes, distracts from worries and allows for self-expression.

» **Space** and peace calm stress chemicals and relax the mind.
» **Exercise** releases feel-good endorphins, boosts energy and reduces stress.
» Regular and good-quality **sleep** reduces stress levels and improves well-being.
» **Team sport** improves social bonding and helps to let off emotional steam.
» **Family games** promote bonding, improve self-control and morality and are fun.
» Being **outdoors** promotes feelings of well-being.
» Accurate **goal setting** reduces negativity and disappointment.
» A job gives a sense of purpose and **financial** reward.
» Family **mealtimes** offer social bonding, positive interaction and spontaneous discussion.

HIRING THE RIGHT SORT OF PARENT

If you are facing challenging situations with your teenager, but find that life settles back into a reasonably calm routine for periods of time before the next round of troubles, this suggests that the child is moving quite well between the settled and unsettled systems, without getting stuck in the latter.

The main thing to bear in mind is that all behaviour is driven by underlying emotions. Negative behaviours like sulking, disobedience, being constantly demanding or mean to siblings are all red flags indicating emotional overload. This results in parents focusing on the bad behaviour. But remind yourself that bad behaviour is offering you vital information about what else might be going on. You know your child and your instinct will be invaluable.

PICKING UP THE SIGNALS

If you're starting to see difficult behaviour around the ages of 13, 14 or 15, with your first child it can be hard to assess how much is just normal teenage ups and downs or whether it is the consequence of something else. If a child is quiet this does not necessarily mean that all is well. In the same way, if a child is demanding and confrontational this does not necessarily indicate that things are not right.

Often, what will put it on one side of this line or the other will be the intensity and frequency of the behaviour. If certain triggers always set off certain reactions, then the concern is that this might be getting wired into the brain as a habit.

ARE THEY LIVING IN A TIDY BEDROOM?

Looking back to the settled and unsettled behaviour systems we covered in Chapters 2 and 4, a teenager's developing mind could be seen to hover in the panic zone and then fall either into the settled system or be tipped into the unsettled system. See your child's mind like the state of their bedroom.

> » **Extremely disorganised and utterly chaotic with clothes escaping from wardrobes and dirty washing taking root on the carpet.** You can barely access this child's room, or touch base with them, because their avoidant strategies ensure that they are sleeping until lunchtime, out with friends till all hours and not falling back into their messy bed until well after your bedtime.

There is a sense of 'Confront me if you can catch me' along with a sense of avoidance of responsibility or taking stock, **or**

» **Extremely tidy and obsessively uncluttered so that the wardrobe doors are clicked tightly shut and withholding all clues as to what's going on.** The bed is crease-free, squeaky clean and the whole feel is of total airbrushed perfection. There is a sense of 'Stepping out of line would be scary' as well as a fear of losing control with disorder.

The first bedroom state is being maintained by an out-of-control mind, the second by an overly controlled mind. Both extremes on the spectrum suggest concealed feelings of insecurity and fear.

ASSESSING THE LIE OF THE LAND

Apart from having your antennae alert, it is also helpful to take stock of the world your children are living in. Those of you with children from around Year Six up to university age may recognise some of the following problems that you or your children are facing:

» Anxiety
» Fear of failure
» Pressure to succeed
» Upheaval/change
» Stress
» Depression
» Fitting in and keeping up with peers

» Moods
» Behaviour such as rudeness/disrespect
» Being uncooperative or lethargic
» Tiredness
» Image (media driven)
» Materialism
» Money
» Letting go
» Boundaries/punishing
» Alcohol
» Drugs
» Eating habits
» Pornography
» Excessive screen usage

It is a sobering list and a reminder of what we are all up against on a daily basis. Take some time to check out how things are for you, your child and their environment to see if anything is waving a flag at you.

Me the Parent

Start with yourself and carry out a quick 'Where am I?' inventory because how you are will directly impact your child (e.g. family, divorce, moving house, work, new partner, finances, new schools, health, university). What level am I at on my personal Richter stress scale? Ask yourself the following questions:

» How am I coping with my work/home life balance?
» Am I stressed and are my underlying emotions contagious to those close to me? In other words, is the whole family going down with my virus?

» Is my teenager's behaviour within the realms of acceptable and normal and therefore tolerable to me?
» Do I tend to protect them from hurt, disappointment or things they find difficult?
» Do I let them get away with things that I should put my foot down about?
» Are alarm bells ringing? Do I see evidence of frequent trips to temptation alley?
» Am I meeting my teenager's needs?

My Child

Follow this with a 'Where is my child?' inventory (e.g. pressured, challenged, struggling, depressed, changes, traumas, upheavals, disappointments, fear, shame, anxiety, anger). Ask yourself the following questions:

» What is going on in my teenager's world?
» Are they coping when things go wrong, e.g. no foot stamping, shouting or sulking?
» Does my child need to anaesthetise, escape or avoid emotional pain in order to cope? E.g. gaming, Facebook, partying?
» If something helped ease their emotional angst or helped to alter mood, what would my child have a tendency towards? (Dieting? Drinking? Defiance?)
» Are they taking responsibility and looking after themselves?

Environmental factors – home and school

Also think about your child's world. Might they feel:

» Not in control of life/decisions/problems?

» Not able to tolerate limits and boundaries (e.g. rebels against rules)?
» Insecure with peer group/not keeping up/not being included?
» Vulnerable to peer pressure in order to fit in?
» Sad, angry or scared as a result of any changes/losses? E.g. divorce, new house, new school, friends, leaving school, bereavement.
» Overly protected and less able to manage their new independent status?
» Abandoned by busy or preoccupied adults?
» Unduly pressured, controlled or criticised?
» Not up to the mark (work/looks/achievements)?
» Anxious about growing up and career decisions?
» Depressed following a trauma/accident/illness or because they do no exercise?
» A need to escape, e.g. by using their Xbox or computer?

Any of the above may cause your child to be in their unsettled system and in need of your engagement.

Remember that branching out into the wider world will involve cutting ties to home in order to establish social connections and a dependence on peers. Experimentation is a part of this quest. However, peer pressure is something to watch because attitudes among a peer group or school community can be contagious and fuel dysfunctional practices that can spread alarmingly quickly (see page 61). This can make dysfunctional strategies seem normal among a group, for instance an over-reliance on social media, viewing online porn or self-harming.

CHAPTER KEY POINTS

» The teen brain is dependent on dopamine during the restructuring process. It is triggered in the brain following novel, fun, exciting pastimes, resulting in feelings of get-up-and-go.

» Good experiences result in feeling successful and motivated. Thrilling risk-taking results in extreme emotional and behavioural highs and lows.

» Regular exposure to good experiences establishes these as long-term behavioural habits. The same applies to negative ones.

» Teenagers' ability to stay on track will depend on their genetic pre-disposition (DNA) and on what life throws at them. Healthy coping strategies help, as does a supportive relationship with a parent.

» Assessing the lie of the land for yourself and your child gives you clues as to where to focus your firepower.

CHAPTER 6

UNDERSTANDING THE MORE CHALLENGING TEENAGE BEHAVIOURS, HABITS AND PASTIMES

Good habits formed at youth make all the difference ...
We are what we repeatedly do. Excellence, then,
is not an act, but a habit.
Aristotle, philosopher

What we are going to tackle now is how a coping strategy can insidiously become a habit, a need or a dependency and how for some it can go the extra mile into a full-blown addiction. We know that the brain's RC is designed to encourage learning and trying out new things. However, given half a chance it will be led astray and hijacked by pleasurable bad habits or behaviours because it is programmed to want more of what feels good and what works.

Coping strategies occupy a wide spectrum. They range from the unsettled fight/flight/freeze behaviours covered in Chapter 4 (see page 69), through to the dysfunctional activities available from temptation alley (smoking, drinking alcohol, disorganised eating, taking marijuana, legal highs and illegal drugs), to the healthy ones we refer to in Chapter 5. *This chapter concentrates on temptation alley.*

Many of the strategies from temptation alley illustrated below could start out as fairly harmless experimentation, but might gather an intensity or persistence with your child.

Frequent indulgence indicates varying levels of anxiety and difficulty in dealing with the emotional impact of daily life. The key thing for us as parents is to help teenagers while they are

Anxiety triggers negative coping strategies

still in our care. We can do this by raising awareness, theirs and ours, in order to help them develop better ways of processing their emotions, and to develop impulse control and future self-discipline. This will be covered towards the end of this chapter and there is more help in Chapters 8 and 9.

THERE MAY BE TROUBLE AHEAD

This is how it starts to go wrong. The teenager feels out of sorts and the brain's RC seeks to boost and realign dopamine, serotonin and other feel-good biochemical levels in the body through:

» Attention- and security-seeking behaviours **or**
» Stimulating, exciting or letting-off-steam activities **or**
» Withdrawing, isolating or numbing pastimes.

These strategies trigger internal change either by upping mood and boosting energy leaving the child feeling more confident, excited, carefree and alert, or by downing mood through anaesthetising or zoning out.

THE DOPAMINE JUNKIE

Any activity that gets dopamine flowing through the RC system will be laid down in the memory files as a useful supplier to be called upon next time levels are dwindling. Regular exposure to experiences that feed the supply become learnt behaviours in the same way as riding a bike or driving a car. So where the chosen activity is marijuana, vodka, Call Of Duty, cutting or bingeing, this is laying the vulnerable teenage brain open to establishing these as strategies to satisfy increased dopamine requirements.

DANGERS OF OVERDOSING ON THE QUICK FIX

Regular exposure to, or overdoses of, any substance or activity that offers a significant change in mood, be it to excite or to offer relief, ram-raids the brain's undeveloped and malleable RC. These experiences tinker with the brain's machinery and restructuring work by forcing it to start to manufacture much more dopamine than it really needs.

HOW DO HABITS TIP INTO BRAIN ADDICTION?

Neuroimaging has now shown how these activities or strategies affect the brain. Many of the activities mentioned in the paragraphs above represent risk and novelty to the excitable teenage brain (think cocaine hit). *Where the brain is forced to process ambushes of highs and lows, addiction is on the cards.* This is because what the brain should be adapting to during these years is natural levels of dopamine that are both manufactured and released into the teenage brain while participating in the sorts of healthy coping strategies outlined in Chapter 5.

ADDICTION IS DOWN TO KEYS AND LOCKS

Dopamine works on a key and lock principle. In order that the dopamine (key) can do its transmitting, it needs a receptor (lock) to attach itself to. If the floodgates in your teenager's brain keep opening as a result of big nights out or pleasurable experiences and releasing more dopamine into the RC, the brain is forced to manufacture more locks.

Like hungry chicks, the locks are demanding and they cry out for their favourite dopamine tipple. Their requests become harder and harder to ignore and over time this pattern causes the brain to restructure itself in order to accommodate all the extra

dopamine keys. The pliable teen brain is particularly vulnerable to adapting in this way.

REMEMBER, REMEMBER

The memory plays its part, helping to establish the habit – good or bad – by producing a small shot of dopamine at the merest whiff of its favourite activity. So if clubbing, a certain crowd, the pub or thinking about sex stimulates a teen to feel the frisson, the brain jumps about with its hand in the air saying, 'I know, I know what to do!' The effect of this is to drive your teenager, without a backwards glance, towards their fix of choice because they remember that it worked to help them feel better last time. And the more that activity results in a feel-good or high feeling, the more your teenager is subconsciously motivated to continue to seek that activity.

HOW THE BRAIN PATHWAYS ARE ESTABLISHED

The bitter reality of addiction is that it establishes itself slowly and insidiously. The RC likes novelty, but each bout of indulgence is slightly less exciting than the last, triggering less dopamine. But less dopamine means hungrier locks and so the stakes need upping in order to satisfy the growing demand. This is when higher levels are needed to feed the plethora of receptors (locks) that have now been manufactured.

The teenage RC is now in full cry, obsessively demanding more of the high associated with its new-found pleasure. Brain 3's rationality, logic and calm reason (or helpful health tips) are firmly overruled.

THE EFFECTS OF THE HIGHS AND LOWS

When the heady sessions of binge and overindulgence are over, your teenager hits the ground with a thud. The result of pillaging the brain's own positive chemical supplies is that teenagers are

SEEKING HELP

If you suspect that your teenager's negative coping strategies may be taking a hold, it is important to **seek professional help.** If you feel that the problem is in the early stages, there are a host of organisations dedicated to providing practical help and advice in dealing with these behaviours (see pages 221–6). Counselling can also be effective and the counselling websites listed on page 221 will help direct you to a suitable practitioner. **If the problem is more pronounced, however, seek advice from your GP without delay.**

left feeling physically exhausted and mentally depleted, resulting in lethargy and heightened levels of anxiety and depression. Our teenagers may tell us that their drinking levels are normal or that everyone is doing *x* or *y*. However, different habits have different effects on the user and the degree of impact is difficult to predict. The risk is not knowing whether the effects and damage will be short or long term. Long-term damage to the brain can include mental illness, clinical depression and psychosis, not to mention the physiological health risks.

WHAT WOULD BEING NOT OKAY LOOK LIKE AND HOW DO THESE COPING STRATEGIES HELP?

It is inevitable that teenagers will slip on banana skins en route to adulthood. What they need to be able to do is pick themselves up, dust themselves down and continue on the journey, wiser for the mishap and more aware of future pitfalls. *Learning this now means that this is the blueprint that they will take with them into adulthood.* Warning signs that danger may lie ahead might be if you notice that your teenager:

» Does not handle difficulties well.
» Cannot think clearly and find solutions to dilemmas.
» Is not able to exercise self-control.
» Gets easily stuck in a rut.
» Tends to overdo it and not stick to limits.

These teenagers are likely to be more vulnerable to seeking and developing a prop or crutch (such as those listed in the table on pge 118) in order to cope and live with their inner emotional chaos. *Teenagers will experiment, but anything that looks like it is creeping towards regular usage should ring alarm bells.*

TRIGGERS AND NEGATIVE COPING STRATEGIES

Emotional trigger	Possible negative coping strategy
Feeling stressed and edgy	Gaming may offer an escape route
Feeling overwhelmed/can't cope	Emotional outbursts may help to let off steam
Feeling isolated/lonely	Facebook may offer distraction
Feeling exhausted and irritable	Food may offer comfort
Feeling disappointed by image	Shopping may help to feel better about self
Feeling frustrated	A cigarette may distract from the pain
Feeling pressured by social gatherings	Alcohol may help to drown the anxiety
Feeling inhibited	Drugs may trigger pleasurable feelings
Feeling uncertain about the opposite sex	Internet porn may satisfy curiosity and desire
Feeling depressed/low	Risky gambling may give a momentary high

HOW THE STRATEGIES WORK

The internal self-regulation dial, which we looked at in Chapter 1 (see page 13), fluctuates like central heating during the day. Emotional triggers grounded in anger, sadness and fear may send the dial up to seven or eight, whereas feeling calm, confident and reassured may bring it down to three or four. Bad stress (see page 54) is when the dial is set at the seven or eight level, leaving the body alert and ready for action 24/7, when there is no need for it to be so. The coping strategies cause the release of calming oxytocin or happy serotonin or feel-good dopamine. Nicotine, alcohol and many recreational drugs cause the release of dopamine into the system, elevating mood, increasing energy and feelings of well-being, and serve to numb or anaesthetise. Controlled eating offers calm control in an emotional world that is all at sea and starving the body of carbohydrates causes the release of feel-good brain chemicals that numb emotional angst. Risky behaviour offers a rush of adrenalin and excitement.

Whatever the strategy, they all have a positive effect on mood in the short term and so the chosen strategy becomes a way of managing dilemmas when they rear their ugly heads.

LIVING IN A FANTASY WORLD

Frustration, disappointment, sadness or having overinflated or unrealistic goals can help fuel perfectionist or obsessive tendencies. The mental drive here is persistence, either for achieving excellence or for getting what they want. What they find when they get there are yet more goals, which result in continual disappointment and a growing sense of failure that erodes their self-esteem.

Conversely, if your child is more prone to a passive mindset they may feel that any effort is pointless because no matter what they do nothing is going to change. This can also result in low self-esteem and adopting habits that keep them within their comfort zone, numbing the subconscious negative feelings. Cannabis and alcohol do this by acting as downers, whereas other drugs act as uppers by raising spirits and result in feeling like the life and soul of the party.

Fear, anxiety or sadness tend to lie at the heart of all the following bad habits.

SMOKING REGULARLY

Nicotine is a poisonous and addictive drug. Every inhalation stimulates the body to produce its own chemicals, for example dopamine and adrenalin. The good feeling may help soothe a teenager who is overwhelmed by social anxiety and a need to feel included and look cool. Like any highly addictive habit, the effects are short-lived, leaving the body craving more. It has similar effects to alcohol, triggering highs and lows. Weight-conscious teenage girls also welcome its effect on suppressing appetite. It is often the first port of call for experimentation by young teenagers, but the younger they start, the harder it is to quit.

Looking through some of the 7,000 chemicals found in cigarettes (including cyanide and ammonia) makes sobering reading.

What you can do:
 » Raise your child's awareness of the content of cigarettes and the risks to their health.
 » Reflect on any underlying causes that might be prompting your child's craving or need for motivating and feel-good dopamine.
 » Avoid turning a blind eye to the developing habit.
 » Make it difficult to smoke at home, even outside in the garden.
 » If you are funding their habit, ask yourself if you are happy to do so.

ALCOHOL

Ethanol is an intoxicating and poisonous ingredient found in alcoholic drinks. Alcohol affects every cell in the body and causes dehydration. Every organ suffers more serious damage too, for example the skin/complexion, liver and vulnerable teenage brain all take a big hit. If the brain were a white muslin square, the alcohol damage would look like burn marks in the fabric. The sobering reality is that the damage never repairs. A drinking spree scrambles logic, planning, decision-making and judgement, so it often lies at the root of high jinx. But it also impacts long-term cognition, memory and attention span so when you consider that this is your teenager's state-of-the-art brain in the making, regular heavy drinking is a poor habit of choice.

Like smoking, alcohol triggers the brain to produce a rush of dopamine, making it highly addictive. The effects are short-lived because it depresses the CNS (see page 12). Combine alcohol with a testosterone-fuelled teenager and this results in slumping serotonin levels, often resulting in aggression or low mood.

The teenage brain needs twice as much alcohol to get the same effect as on an adult brain, making big nights prone to huge excesses. Many young people are binge drinking, consuming more than one week's units (17 for a girl and 22 for a boy) in a night. With one unit of alcohol taking one hour to leave the system, driving a car within 24 hours of partying is often risky and dangerous.

Attitudes and culture towards drinking have changed. Sneaking alcohol into someone's house or being sick on their carpet no longer carries embarrassment or shame. With social media spreading messages that getting drunk is hilarious, copycat behaviour among teenagers is rife.

What you can do:

» Don't get your teenager accustomed to alcohol. Early experimentation is irresponsible because it conditions the brain to want more dopamine via this route.

» Hold out for no drinking in your house for as long as you can. When your teens do start, explain why you limit supplies.

» Don't turn a blind eye if their drinking at home with their friends exceeds your limits.

» Check that they have eaten before they go out.

» Get them to talk about the negative effects of alcohol on others so that they start to develop their own views and limits.

» Talk to other parents about plans for social gatherings. Don't be afraid to be a killjoy.

» Keep your own excesses out of view of impressionable teenagers.

DISORGANISED EATING HABITS

Disordered eating can sometimes affect those with perfectionist tendencies and can develop from an unrealistic need to have a media-perfect airbrushed body. A perfectionist's attitude springs from a distorted belief that beauty and thinness will bring happiness and can be achieved through controlled eating.

What can also happen is that a young person accidentally discovers that controlling their food intake and developing rituals around eating becomes a way of feeling as though they have regained control of their otherwise chaotic emotions. Self-monitored eating habits may also help them keep a lid on their unsettled panic, fear and rage.

Bulimia

A cycle of binge eating followed by self-induced vomiting is characteristic of a bulimic. The pattern tends to be a closely guarded secret and because it does not necessarily result in weight loss it is less immediately noticeable than anorexia. It is motivated by a need for control and it is the eating ritual and feeling of being full that becomes soothing and offers a distraction from the other anxieties a child might be feeling.

If the home environment is difficult or tense, for example, this can trigger feelings of fear and loss and magnify the sense of being out of control. Controlled eating rituals give a temporary feeling of being back in the driving seat, releasing soothing, calming biochemicals into the system that the brain registers as a strategy that works. The next time the child feels panicked and craves comfort, they risk turning to this remembered bingeing/vomiting strategy, which is how the cycle to dependency starts.

Anorexia

Anorexia is much more visible than bulimia in that it is accompanied by more obvious and often acute weight loss. Those suffering from it have a very unrealistic sense of their weight and although painfully thin will often see an overweight image in the mirror. Feelings of anxiety and loss of control also prevail, along with a difficulty with expressing emotions. Anorexics are often good, compliant and high-achieving perfectionists and find it difficult to adjust to the reality of things going wrong. If a child has always been cushioned from failure or mishap, or overly praised, strong feelings of powerlessness or shame may ignite at the first whiff of failure.

What you can do:

» Notice if your teenager has difficulty identifying or expressing how they feel.

» If your child sets very high goals, help them reset them to a level that is realistic and achievable.

» Appreciate and acknowledge their personal qualities rather than simply their achievements or looks.

» If home life is going through a rough patch, encourage your child not to spend too much time isolated in their bedroom.

» Don't hide disagreements from your child as they are opportunities for them to witness rupture and repair in relationships.

» Make sure family mealtimes are pleasurable experiences and that you are role-modelling healthy eating patterns.

If you have a sense that an eating disorder might be under way, visit your doctor and ask for further support. We have also listed some specialist organisations and websites on page 223. The important thing to bear in mind is that the disordered eating pattern is a symptom and not the cause, so focusing solely on this isn't enough. Make sure that a treatment plan addresses solutions and new strategies to alleviate and express underlying emotions as well.

USING CANNABIS

Cannabis conjures up fairly benign images of flower power and the 1960s. But this belies today's much more serious reality of stronger varieties of these drugs. In some cases, regular use has resulted in paranoia, anxiety and even psychosis.

Teenagers who find reality hard to cope with and who need to blot out their emotional world find that cannabis helps in distorting and dulling perceptions and emotional pain. Using these drugs in the teen years is risky because the drugs work to hijack areas of the brain under development and have a long-term impact on cognition and memory. The younger the habit starts, and the longer it persists, the worse the memory impairment. Motivation is another casualty of regular use.

What you can do:

- » Don't be fooled into comparing today's cannabis with the sort of dope you may have smoked as a teenager.
- » Help your child to understand the risks and be realistic. Do this by counteracting any discussions about these being harmless.
- » Remind your child about its impact on their ability to think and remember things.
- » State clearly to them that these drugs are illegal in the UK.
- » Be vigilant to the reality that experimentation can quickly lead to regular usage due to the drug's addictive qualities.
- » If you sense that your teenager is smoking cannabis, encourage them to see a counsellor to deal with the underlying emotions that are fuelling the habit.

USING LEGAL HIGHS

The pathways of addiction are the same regardless of whether the favoured habit is legal or illegal. There are many illegal drugs such as cannabis, Ecstasy, ketamine and so forth alongside the legal ones like alcohol, nicotine and other legal highs. They all result in the brain manufacturing more keys and locks, which are the building blocks of addiction.

The insidious sales message to young people is that legal highs are free of risk. The reality is that the drugs are being manufactured so quickly in order to keep ahead of legislation that they are neither regulated nor tested. Strengths may vary hugely from one batch to the next and young people are little more than human guinea pigs in the club drug scene. Another temptation is that legal highs are cheap. For example, laughing gas (almost as popular as cannabis) is available for a few pounds.

The culture among many young people is that everyone is doing legal highs – at festivals, during gap years, at university or nightclubs – so it's normal, chillax. But we are back to the same reality that the dopamine frenzy generated by legal highs hijacks the RC and renders Brain 3 woefully unable to exert control.

What you can do:

» Spell out the difference between 'legal' and 'safe' to clarify any misconceptions about the drugs being harmless.

» Remind them that 'legal' is not the same as 'regulated' and that there is no consistency or control over the content of varying batches.

» Talk about drugs such as ketamine, which started out as a legal high but is now illegal and is now known to produce serious side effects including irreparable damage to the bladder, sometimes resulting in incontinence.

» Start talking to them and educating them and yourself before they reach the age where they might experiment.

» Wise up to the festival scene and check out your

teenager's attitudes and plans before they receive your sanction to go.

» Don't ignore any signs of paranoia (extreme irrational fear), raised levels of anxiety (unrelenting and uncontrollable worry) or panic attacks. Seek medical help immediately.

Look at websites (there are some examples on pages 223–4) and find out about legal and illegal drugs, especially the cheaper ones, and the side effects of many of the chemically engineered substances available for legal use. This helps you to be as objective as possible on the whole issue and may help your teen to think and talk things through with you. Are they addictive, for instance? Are they linked to psychosis? Could they exacerbate levels of anxiety/paranoia in a child who is already low in confidence/self-esteem? Is depression a side effect? Asking these sorts of questions gives you authority and knowledge when you embark on your conversation with your child. Your child needs to know what they might be getting themselves into both in the short and long term.

OTHER DRUGS

Here is a quick outline of other common drugs and their effects. We have included the better-known ones, but there are many drugs out there, so this list is by no means exhaustive.

Stimulant drugs or uppers

These are amphetamine based and work by upping activity in the reward centre. They give lots of energy, enabling users to stay up all night, so are used at festivals and in clubs. However, they can also exacerbate any aggressive tendencies in users. Cocaine was the daddy of party drugs, but cheaper alternatives like Ecstasy (MDMA) and mephedrone were launched as legal highs. They have now been made illegal. Legal alternatives are marketed as Ecstasy-based herbal highs.

Anaesthetics or hallucinogenic drugs

These drugs give a happy, intense and euphoric feeling, while distorting sensory perceptions. LSD and magic mushrooms are the old established ones, but ketamine (a horse tranquilliser) is one of the new drugs.

Opiate drugs or downers (depressants)

Opiates produce a state of euphoria and relaxation by sedating and calming the brain like morphine or codeine. Examples are heroin, alcohol and marijuana.

Medication and self-medication

Partying hard often results in illness (e.g. fresher's flu, glandular fever, laryngitis) and a whole generation of young are reputedly using prescription and over-the-counter drugs as pick-me-ups. Some of the popular ones are listed below, along with the effects if dosage and instructions are abused, but bear in mind that there are many more, this list is not comprehensive:

» Ibuprofen washed down with large quantities of alcohol results in stomach bleeding.
» Stronger painkillers such as codeine combined with alcohol increases drowsiness.
» Cough medicines containing dextromethorphan (DXM) are harmless when used for the intended purpose. However, when combined with alcohol they become addictive and can be hallucinogenic.

» ADHD (Attention Deficit Hyperactivity Disorder) drugs (which work like Ritalin) and caffeine-based pills and drinks promote alertness and focus, and are used to help stay up for long hours, to party and to study. This short-lived high is followed by a dramatic slump in energy.

» Sleeping pills have a knockout effect but they interfere with the body's natural patterns, making it difficult to fall asleep without them. They are highly addictive.

What you can do:

» Is your child frequently buying over-the-counter remedies or visiting the doctor for more prescriptions? Do you know what they are buying and taking?

» Is your child able to say no to friends and opt to have a quiet night in when feeling below par or do they keep going until they virtually collapse?

» Look out for evidence of any medication being regularly used (e.g. laxatives).

If you feel your teen may be self-medicating, alert them to the side effects of prolonged use of over-the-counter or prescription medicines.

SELF-HARMING BEHAVIOURS

Self-harm includes cutting, burning or scratching the skin to cause physical hurt. The perceived benefits from pursuing self-harming behaviours are similar to those of many of the other coping strategies. The internal biochemical responses to self-inflicted pain provide feelings of comfort and anaesthetise the mind. They can also become a strategy for managing and regulating overwhelming and uncontainable feelings.

While caring adults and support services throw up their hands in horror over the habit, what gets sidelined is the reason why this child needed to reach out for this coping strategy in the first place. Was it their low-level anxiety as a result of life at home, their fear of failure at school, their low self-worth due to image or their perfectionist tendencies due to unnaturally high goal setting? If you are facing a self-harming issue with your teenager, thinking about these possible causes will help you focus on the real problem underneath. So if, for example, your instinct tells you that your child's anxiety is being stoked by fear of failure, you can try and alleviate this by reassurance and helping to modify expectations. The important thing to bear in mind is that the coping strategy, just as with disordered eating on page 124. (See also pages 224–5.)

What you can do:
- » Trust your gut instinct. If you sense that a self-harming behaviour is being used, try to open up a conversation with your child, even though this will be difficult to do.
- » Gently encourage your child to approach and express feelings rather than bottling them up.
- » Show them how to do this by talking about feelings yourself – your own, those of a character in a book or film, or your observations of a stranger.
- » Help them to link their behaviour to their feelings (underlying anxiety/insecurity) so they begin to see that their behaviour is a coping strategy.

If you think your child might be self-harming, in addition to any help that you give it is important to seek counselling and consult your GP for medical advice. Remember that the self-harming behaviour points to an underlying difficulty with emotional expression and containment.

Many of the habits and pastimes discussed above carry a high risk of causing harm to your teenager and others. The outcome is almost always destructive – to morale, esteem, health of body and mind, and to relationships. The concern is when a young person becomes unable to function without their chosen strategy to regulate or boost their mood. This is where it is vital that we as parents step in early to try and help them discover some positive strategies to which they can turn when in need.

TIME FOR PARENTS TO WISE UP

It can be frightening when things feel like they are beginning to slide and it is tempting to turn a blind eye and hope your teenager will grow out of it. *However, if underlying issues are left to fester the coping strategy is likely to develop into a much bigger problem.* If any of the issues we have discussed in this chapter raise alarm bells for you, now is the time to put the stick away ('It's my fault, I'm a bad parent') and focus energy instead on finding constructive ways to help your child. Some parents would prefer not to talk to their child about their habits because it may end in confrontation. Alternatively, they may risk becoming unpopular if they lay down some limits and boundaries. Or they may be considered pathetic, annoying and not as cool as other parents. Confronting a problem with your teenager is not easy but along with the specific suggestions in each of the above sections, bear in mind that:

» Facing demons and helping your child to overcome what is really troubling them develops future resilience. It is not always possible to avoid traumas or upheavals in a child's life but it is an opportunity for you to help them to find functional ways of coping that will become lifelong habits.

» Sometimes traumas going back as far as preverbal days resurface as unsettled behaviour while the brain tidies up its filing system.

» Sometimes bad behaviour has been on a slow burn for years but it gathers intensity during the teenage period.

» Teenagers have a tendency to believe what they want to believe so be prepared to face resistance when you broach difficult conversations.

» Kick-start general conversations using newspaper articles, stories from friends, film characters, celebrities or videos on YouTube.

» Teenagers are heavily influenced by their peers. Don't be relegated to the subs bench. Stay involved and informed about their interests, attitudes and pastimes.

» Choose your words carefully. If they sense criticism, they will shut down.

CHAPTER KEY POINTS

» Coping strategies, whether healthy or negative, work by triggering the release of feel-good dopamine in the brain, resulting in positive mood change.

» Teenagers need to experiment and take risks as they grow up. Be vigilant to any extremes.

» If a bad habit becomes a regular strategy for coping when things are not going well, this paves the way to it becoming a brain addiction.

» The key to comprehending negative coping strategies is to understand what has prompted your teenager to reach out for it (perhaps loss, fear or anger).

» Before negative coping strategies become a necessary or regular occurrence, try and wise up and engage your teenager in discussion.

» When things get out of hand, seek professional help and support.

CHAPTER 7

WHAT IS GOING ON IN THE DIGITAL AND TECHNOLOGICAL WORLD?

*The familiar fixture of our households today:
the glassy-eyed, monosyllabic adolescent in deep dialogue
with their screen….The question I want to ask is not
what we can do with the Web, but rather what will it
do to us in terms of our identity?….Is it not marginally
reminiscent of a small child saying 'Look at me,
look at me Mummy! Now I've put my sock on.'*
Baroness Susan Greenfield, scientist, writer and broadcaster

Like it or loathe it, digital mania has swept the world in the last decade or so and is here to stay. This generation of young screenagers has been plunged into the technology and digital revolution. Although there are undeniable benefits – access to information, instant communication, keeping in touch through social networks – there is also mounting evidence of the negative long-term impact technology may have on children, both younger and older. Many are spending long hours immersed in mindless screen-based entertainment or in overstimulating screen activities resulting in a double whammy of damage. This comes from the process of spending endless hours in front of a screen (gaming, watching TV, texting/communicating) as well as the content of some of the material (for example on porn or pro-eating disorder websites, gambling, media influence and general marketing).

Both the process and the content play havoc with brain function and addiction pathways, as well as the mind's evolving attitudes, values and behaviour. In short, your child's developing mental health and overall persona. In addition, there is concern about the potentially damaging effect of a child spending 24/7 in the

close vicinity of electromagnetic radiation emitted from their laptop or mobile, which can affect their sleep patterns.

THE PROS AND CONS OF THE INTERNET

We know that vulnerable young brains are shaped by their daily preoccupations and beliefs, which means that children are inevitably going to be moulded by their passive or active involvement with screens, whether they are being used for communication, information or learning.

THE INTERNET SOCIETY

As a source of knowledge the internet broadcasts information on a wealth of issues straight into your home, much of which is useful, interesting and harmless. *But there is also an insidious side where it acts as a powerful vehicle for communicating emerging attitudes and lifestyles, some of which may be of concern to you.* The medium allows these ideas – sometimes negative ones – to be spread quickly, like a virus, among a generation of young who are eager to seek out, discover and learn new things.

Today's young are strongly influenced and governed by the media and what it promotes, even more than by the wisdom of the older generation. As a result, we are all as parents likely to be facing a seismic shift in attitudes and values from our children. Given this it's a good idea to keep yourself in the loop. Be aware of what is on offer on the internet and the television and use precious time with your children to have spontaneous conversations that will reveal their tastes. Children are naturally curious and their minds are like sponges, but some of what they discover online might need realigning with real opinions and attitudes so that your teenager grows up with a wider and more balanced viewpoint.

One reason the internet world is so alluring is that it is like a community of its own which, like a society, is built on understandings and beliefs that help to shape the culture and behaviour of the group.

INTERNET SUPPORT

Teenagers are at a stage where they are often emotionally fragile and have insecurities about their image, making the internet even more seductive for its escapism, reassurance, support or help. There is information on just about everything – how to lose weight, drugs, sex and unfortunately there are even websites on suicide. This presents obvious dangers to young, impressionable minds and if a child is out of sorts emotionally and unable to get help from parents, family, school or friends, they are even more likely to turn to the internet. A child who might have a natural tendency to withdraw when under pressure, for instance, may seek support or answers online. The internet poses as a perfect forum to draw in young people who are lonely, withdrawn, depressed, feeling out of control, helpless or with poor social skills and are seeking help. Teenagers can easily slip into feeling isolated and lonely so try and make sure this isn't happening by encouraging them to connect and engage with people and have lots of interests.

Websites can be a double-edged sword. Those on eating disorders, for instance, appear to be helpful and kind, providing online forums and groups where other like-minded people can virtually congregate and network. The result for the vulnerable child is that they are whisked into a world where they suddenly feel secure, included, normal and belong to this new cyber family. Without having to express weaknesses and face up to them in the real world, they can hide behind the comfort and veil of anonymity in an online world.

COMMUNICATING AND SOCIALISING ONLINE

Humans are inherently social beings with an inbuilt biological need and drive to connect and communicate and to establish meaningful relationships because they offer good feelings of security, trust, safety and closeness. *The rise in screens has revolutionised the way we communicate, displacing hours that might previously have been spent communicating face-to-face with all the positive benefits that socialising and genuine friendship bring.*

Laptops, mobiles and tablets play an integral part in how our society functions and most of our communication, socialising and entertainment involve a screen of some sort. Certain screen-based activities will have an observable impact on your child's personality and some children will be more adversely affected than others so keep an eye out for how each child is responding.

EARLY-WARNING SIGNS

Early-warning signs that things are heading in the wrong direction can be detected from:

» **Changing behaviour pre or post screen-based activities** – demanding, aggressive, not sleeping, moody, lethargic or uncooperative.
» **Negative language** – 'I need to...', 'I have to always...', 'I want to...', 'I'm obsessed about...', 'I'm addicted to...', 'I'm tired...'.

SOCIAL ANXIETY

Beware of chicken and egg. Because your child feels insecure or anxious they may find comfort by withdrawing to solitary screen-based activities, reducing face-to-face communication. *However, the irony is that the reduced human interaction that results from this kind of socialising further reduces feelings of security, trust and safety and a negative cycle develops.* The less secure a child feels, the more they turn to technology for their social fix and the more they do this, the less experience they have of real communication. Indeed, they fit in less well socially and as a result they feel less secure. As parents, we can help guard against this by making sure that they are involved in any social gatherings with family and friends and that they are not making excuses to avoid contact.

Screen-based communication carries a hefty potential for provoking anxiety. Anxiety is triggered by threat, just as it was in the cave people's day, but today's perceived threats are linked to social, rather than physical survival. Even though teenagers were always concerned about what people thought of them prior to the arrival of social networking sites, the difference was that they did not have the rest of the world to compare or compete with. Today's teenagers' airbrushed identities fuels a frantic desire to always look good and to be overly fixated on their own appearance, which can trigger feelings of low self-worth.

An overdependence on technology is a behaviour like any other behaviour you are dealing with. Try and see beyond it to anxiety and fear, which are most often the underlying triggers for all sorts of manifestations of bad behaviour.

The arrival of the internet has meant that today's young are inundated with demands that provoke anxiety about:

» Their media identity and keeping their public image intact.
» Their privacy.
» FOMO (fear of missing out)/inadequacy.
» Having to be on call to respond to incoming demands 24/7.
» Recording and sharing every experience.
» Not having time or freedom to enjoy the moment.

The cyber world is pressurised and may be contributing to a rise in unsettled behaviours, habits and pastimes in your child.

THE POWER OF REAL FRIENDSHIP

A great deal of today's socialising happens with groups forming through message contacts, Facebook connections, links, forums, following or gathering followers, chatlines and online games. These are all ways young people today can feel connected and popular. Communicating online lowers inhibitions and offers the potential for more familiarity so that people feel able to say more than they would face-to-face and a potentially inappropriate relationship can feel seemingly intimate very quickly. However, the written word also has the potential to create misunderstandings and new needy friends may be transient and lack the depth of real friendship. *Face-to-face rapport and non-verbal feedback give a real sense of connection and intimacy that cyber networking cannot replace.*

Making sure that your child has access to a sound base of proper friends is vital. Better still, make sure that your home is a place where young people can congregate, socialise and have fun without being dependent on gaming or TV. You will learn a lot about your child's world by watching how they interact with their peers. Facebook and use of their mobile phone to keep in touch with friends should be seen as a bonus and an addition to real friendship.

It is tempting to think that your child is okay because they are online chatting to friends, but you need to see them with real friends in order to have evidence that they have a solid friendship base. Without this your child may be socially anxious and may actually feel lonely without you realising it. Relationships based on texting or chat rooms and groups may appear to give some comfort to the social anxiety, but it leaves vulnerable teenagers less sociably able.

When today's teenagers hit challenging periods in their lives there is a chance that they may get sucked into a cyber world, which further compounds their unsettled and insecure thoughts, feelings and behaviours. With your child's mental health in the making, be wary of who and what they are turning to for support.

THE ADDICTION POTENTIAL

Screenagers and parents alike joke about being addicted to their screens, be it TV soaps, their Facebook status or checking their phone every few minutes (including during meals, business meetings, lessons and in bed at night). New-age disorders like nomophobia (no-mobile-phone phobia – for this, think separation anxiety, see pages 162–5) are triggered when panic sets in because the perceived lifeline has been severed ('No one can get in touch with me!') along with FOMO should the next social fix be threatened.

In terms of addiction potential it is worth remembering that screen addiction is a genuine disorder (e.g. gaming) and screens are an easy gateway, insidiously posing a very real risk to your teenager (e.g. pornography or gambling) in the same way as alcohol or drugs. The problem is that they are even more readily available 24/7, piped into the home at a reasonably low cost and are sometimes considered a normal (and a necessary, for homework and work) part of life today.

BEING ADDICTED TO SCREENS

Chapter 6 looked at how coping strategies, for instance using alcohol or drugs, can be depended upon to excite (someone who is sad/depressed), calm (someone who is stressed/angry) or numb (someone who is anxious/frightened) and how using these strategies can easily slip into an addictive habit. Some teens are genetically predisposed to anxiety and are more likely to develop a compulsive or addictive coping strategy to quell the emotional ruckus. They may be more vulnerable to a screen-based addiction.

Consider these sobering ways in which needs and habits can creep up:

- » **Addiction** – to spending hours in another world online shopping.
- » **Habit** – of carrying a phone in a pocket and checking emails 24/7.
- » **Compulsion** – to keep gambling, despite the risk.
- » **Dependence** – on phone, resulting in panic when it goes missing.
- » **Need** – to keep revisiting porn sites throughout the day, despite risk of being caught.
- » **Obsession** – of watching certain TV programmes repeatedly for long hours.

» **Craving** – gaming and not stopping, despite hunger or tiredness.

» **Infatuation** – with Facebook and stalking oneself to check the profile is up to the mark.

WHAT'S AVAILABLE IN YOUR HOME?

The majority of screen-based habits have little intrinsic value, yet there is a bewildering array of them on tap. Their value is that they seem to offer something pleasurable and exciting, or they offer a safe haven from the current status quo. So let us look at the most readily accessible and popular screen-based activities as well as the potential downsides of unrestricted access.

Social Networking Sites

Most of us are familiar with the frustration of watching our children anxiously and compulsively checking their updated status throughout the day and broadcasting their every move. Apart from FOMO, they find it more and more difficult to totally switch off and enjoy whatever they are doing privately and in the moment.

Material that should be private and photographs of your child can be broadcast by someone else without permission raising the important issue of the boundary between public and private experience. Distinguishing between these is increasingly hard for today's teenagers and helping them do this is vital if they are to learn the crucial art of saying no when necessary. This is the start of self-policing. As parents, we can help raise their awareness to things that should be private by encouraging them to think about where they would draw the line for themselves. Celebrities and public personalities offer antics and examples that can be helpful in initiating conversations with our teenagers.

Social media also provides a communication platform that may change how you would treat other people, particularly when a group of 'friends' are involved. Studies are being carried out on whether social networking provides new forums for bad social habits (e.g. rudeness, gossip and bitchiness). Your child's Facebook account is likely to be a closely guarded secret and although starting to develop your own identity is a crucial part of growing up, the complete absence of adult guidance leaves this vulnerable to developing in unpleasant ways.

KEEPING TABS

Keeping an eye on what is going on isn't easy. Some parents may choose to befriend their child on Facebook, but children have been known to set up a second account. It is an idea to have an **older person** who your child **likes and respects** (e.g. a sister or cousin) who can keep checking that your child's page **looks okay** and can perhaps gently **point out ill-judged images or comments.**

Future employers often check Facebook in order to get a sense of what sort of person a potential employee is when their guard is down so it is important that teens are not posing as something they are not. Facebook also publicises inappropriate material, which then seems normal to viewers. Keep up with what is going on in the Facebook world and aim to limit the amount of time your child spends on social networking sites.

Eating Disorder Websites

Prior to the internet, the chances of young girls finding information about how to develop an eating disorder were very small. Now there are pro-ana (anorexia) and pro-mia (bulimia) sites creating online forums where like-minded (mostly) girls can congregate and share in-depth tips and advice on dieting, purging, laxative use and so forth, and on how to develop the sort of avoidance strategies to resist proper help or treatment.

Young girls are applauded and encouraged by the online community and offered helpful tips on how to manipulate and deceive adults who might be checking up on their calorie intake. Websites and chat rooms offer mutual admiration forums extolling the virtues of anorexia and bulimia and present them as lifestyle choices rather than unhealthy disorders. The allure of competing for the biggest following particularly draws in isolated and vulnerable teenagers who are struggling with self-esteem at a time when they are forging a new adult image, attitudes and behaviours. With the teenage brain programming itself for adult habits, getting healthy behaviours in place now is crucial.

Although more prevalent in girls, there are increasing numbers of boys developing eating disorders in recent years so arm yourself with information on what is out there for your teens to access (see page 223).

Legal Highs Information Online

Nothing could be easier to access than legal highs. They are marketed online, are readily available on the street and can be conveniently delivered to your door with the postman acting as supplier. Discreetly packaged 'chemical/herbal products' or 'for laboratory use only' or 'not for human consumption' parcels are unlikely to catch parental attention. They are unregulated and untested (see pages 125–7) and teens are exposed to constantly changing websites informing them about the latest must-have pill, so knowing what is being promoted is important for us as parents.

Self-harming Websites

Without going online and seeing them it is hard for parents to believe that there are websites promoting various kinds of deliberate self-harm, such as cutting. Some sites aggressively reject those who quit self-harming, making it difficult for some people to give up the validation and sense of belonging that came from being in the cyber group. This makes it even harder to change their behaviour.

If you feel your child is vulnerable, have a look at these sites so you know what they are peddling. Teenagers who find it difficult to express and stabilise their emotions are particularly vulnerable to turning to self-harm. Anything that parents can do to encourage a child with this tendency not to bottle things up will help protect them from turning to these behaviours. (See also pages 129–31.)

Shopping

Internet shopping presents a huge opportunity to empty the coffers. The thrill of the chase, particularly with auction sites, and the fix of the purchase gives rise to another addiction – the shopaholic. Over time, we condition ourselves to buy stuff in order to feel better, to cheer ourselves up, to treat ourselves or celebrate success. Habits get established when your teenager sees something they must have because everyone else has it. They feel they need it, they convince themselves or you that it will make them feel better and so they (or you) succumb to it. These are all patterns that are using the same pleasure/reward pathways as any other addiction. If we as parents can avoid using material rewards to celebrate success or to compensate for disappointments, we are not conditioning our children to use this habit as a future strategy.

Health Info

Any health concern or out-of-the-ordinary symptom and your teen will turn to the internet to find out all about it. Fragmented and partially understood information often taken out of context further fuels their anxiety and worry and they often jump to the wrong conclusions. Make sure that you take their concerns seriously, sometimes your reassurance and attention may be enough to relieve symptoms, but a trip to the doctor may help to prevent future psychosomatic (mind/body) dramas being so easily triggered. Many of their aches and pains are likely to be lifestyle induced. Help them to prevent future health concerns by linking their actions to consequences.

Gambling

Getting swept up in the excitement and thrill of taking the punt and monetary reward affects the areas in the brain responsible for decision-making, so the ability to stop is impeded. Although women are not immune to the lure of gambling, it appears to draw in more men. Before the male brain has established the ability to link actions to consequences (at about age 24) and the art of self-control, gambling is a real-life problem for many young people. The internet has made it much more accessible and a teenager who is particularly excited by winning or financial gain might be more susceptible to this.

Not only is online gambling now widely advertised and readily available on a mobile 24/7, it is also alarmingly easy to place bets. It offers an escape route from real-life dilemmas so be particularly vigilant if you have a child who needs to zone out from reality. The potential damage is not only losing huge sums of money, but also the serious emotional fallout, including shame and despair. Talking through with children the speed with which losses can accumulate can help them link action to consequence. Once ingrained, gambling is a difficult habit to overcome so if you have concerns about your teenager there is information on gambling support networks and counselling on page 225.

Pornography

There is no escaping the fact that pornography is big business. In the blink of an eye it has been catapulted into an industry with a worldwide turnover of billions. With millions of sites/ pages available online with one click of a mouse, today's parents do not have the comfort of putting off or preventing their child from observing inappropriate pornographic material by simply disposing of the well-thumbed magazine concealed under the mattress.

Parents have many reactions when the subject is raised, ranging from naughty childish smirks ('A bit of fun', 'Never did us any harm') to taking the moral high ground ('People who look at porn are debauched, it should be banned!') to revulsion and head in the sand ('Disgusting, I don't want to know'). Whatever your values or attitudes to pornography, the uncomfortable truth about what has changed is:

> » The age at which young (often) boys are accessing the material (from around nine).
> » The number of children who are exposed to age-inappropriate material.

» The volume of material available online (around 52 million pages in UK).

» The way it is presented, in movie format, not photos.

» The content and breadth, which is highly explicit, barely legal, often violent, diverse, degrading, impersonal, unrealistic and traumatic.

» The accessibility 24/7 on the move and at school or home.

» The effect it is having on values, attitudes and an understanding of sex for a generation of young people.

» The normalisation and acceptance of underage/ varied/impersonal/non-committal sexual practices.

» The acceptability of the attitudes of a few that are spreading like a virus via social/media networks to become widespread social values.

Healthy sexual development for teenagers

Hormone changes, natural curiosity, exploration and experimentation should fire up a young person's sexual systems (see page 29) in their brain. This starts to happen at around the age of eight to ten but continues into puberty. Slowly, over time, their sexual identity should develop prior to their first sexual experience. Developing a sexual ability and orientation, a healthy attitude towards sex and feeling good about having a mutually satisfying relationship are key players in this transition.

Exciting curiosity

Learning how to do something well involves curiosity and experimentation. Hands-on experience fires up the brain's reward centre and the feel-good chemicals help the mind to develop thoughts and beliefs about ability. In terms of learning how to have an intimate relationship, it needs a slow build, involving trial and error, and discovery. Part of the process of building intimacy involves mutual trust, warmth and respect, from which an understanding develops of what is satisfying and works for the two people involved.

Sexual dysfunction

For a young person who has not yet experienced a mutually satisfying relationship, today's online pornographic moving images (rather than still photos in a magazine) short-circuit the establishment of the slow-build arousal pathways in the brain by delivering an instantly gratifying ready-made experience that imprints itself in the memory. The links between the teenage mind and body in this instance are being trained up to only respond to hard-core porn to achieve arousal, anything less just won't float the boat.

It is difficult not to link today's brand of pornography with the sharp rise in reports of sexual dysfunction among young men in their twenties reporting difficulties gaining or maintaining an erection or difficulties with ejaculation. Young men are astonished to connect watching pornography with being sexually inadequate. Long term, there is a risk of addiction, mental illness and persistent physical dysfunction.

Curiosity killed the cat

Online pornography displays lots of different sexual behaviours and practices. It is hard-core, impersonal, fetish, violent or degrading and as parents we should look at a porn site to see what our children are exposed to. The reality is that many of today's adolescents are modelling their sexual behaviour on what they are learning and experiencing online. The younger a boy is when he first looks at porn, the more his sexual expectations will be influenced.

Step forward parents!

Viewing pornography affects girls and boys in different ways. Conversations with sons need to be factual, clear and straightforward. However difficult the subject, we need to alert our teenagers to the detrimental effects of pornography and boys can find it easier if fathers or other important male figures approach the issue. Apart from the physiological impact, it invokes important questions of respect, morality and the abuse of power. Fathers and male figures need to talk to teenage boys not just once, but regularly, because there isn't widespread education on this in schools yet. Divorced parents have a chance to highlight potential pitfalls and regrets, and reflect on relationships generally. Boys need a healthy blueprint of mutual intimacy on which to model their developing attitudes and

SOME HARDCORE FACTS ABOUT PORNOGRAPHY

» It stimulates mirror neurons in the brain, making the experience ripe for replication and copycat behaviour, and even vicarious experiencing of what is viewed online.
» It is linked to provoking sexual dysfunction in boys.
» It promotes narcissistic and selfish ideas about sex.
» Although fewer girls look at online pornography, their attitudes, practices and behaviour are powerfully influenced by expectations among their peers.
» A variety of questionable practices become normalised among teenagers.
» Flagging male libido can result in girls linking this to their low sex appeal, sparking a sharp decline in self-esteem levels.

sexual behaviour. This will help them resist the narcissistic and selfish attitudes fuelled by online pornography.

Girls also need frank conversations about this so that your daughter gathers confidence that she need not feel pressurised to do something she feels uncomfortable with. If your children have had ample opportunity to talk to you about this thorny subject in a no-nonsense way they may have a better understanding about what is acceptable and what is not when they are under pressure and they may feel able to ask you questions rather than form their views based on sometimes dubious online sources.

The effects of online viewing are disturbing and as parents we need to check out what our children might be able to access on the Wi-Fi at home. Wi-Fi access in bedrooms carries obvious risks, so if possible have internet availability only in main rooms so you can casually monitor online activity. Smartphones are harder to police but under-18 filters will help limit what can be viewed. High data usage on phones will also suggest considerable video viewing so if this is happening find out what your child is watching. This will help to support your efforts to be proactive in guiding your child as opposed to hoping that they stumble upon the right path.

It can feel like a hopeless and losing battle to try and keep children away from pornography and its pernicious effects. But ultimately what will help them reject what they see is learning from their parents about the negative aspects of pornography plus witnessing good family relationships with all their complexities.

Gaming

In today's world of gaming, the biochemical highs received by the teenage brain are coming from sedentary and non-motor (physical, sport) activities. Gaming results in a rise in adrenalin

(Mr Fight and Flight, see page 33) and testosterone (see page 34 and below), but if there is no physical release of the high this will impact behaviour and hyperactivity. Most parents say that they notice a downturn in behaviour and mood post-gaming, with a rise in levels of confrontation, aggression, sulking or boredom.

Many parents don't really know how these games pull a child in so a good idea is to test out the more advanced games yourself. Play for an hour and then get someone to turn the game off with a cheerful 'Supper's ready!' Make a mental note of your mood, feelings, behaviour and excitement (adrenalin) levels. How long does it take you to feel calm and how much does the game influence how you view the real world? Now throw into the mix the fact that your child's rational executive controller (the cortex, Brain 3) is not open for business and that the impulsive emotional brain is in control. This will give you an idea of how much more difficult it is for young teenagers to behave sensibly when in the grips of a gaming adrenalin rush and to separate the game's influences from real life. Talk it through with your child and explain some of the processes at work. They may look disinterested, but you will find that most teenagers avidly listen when the subject being discussed is how they function and why.

In terms of time spent playing, if you can agree a plan that your child has to implement you will be encouraging their collaboration and self-discipline. Slowly you want them to take responsibility for how long is an acceptable amount of time to play before mood and behaviour starts to deteriorate.

Get physical

Testosterone levels vary between individuals and levels are raised naturally by physically competitive sport. Testosterone has a direct impact on aggression. Where this is on the football pitch there is a natural outlet to the heightened hormone levels and boys are also learning how to contain anger and tolerate frustration by playing sport, so it is the ideal way to learn to behave well while being in highly competitive situations. Boys need to learn self-management, self-discipline and self-control.

So give your child plenty of opportunity (e.g. through playing family games) to fine-tune their self-regulation dial and let off steam in the safe confines of home. Some teenagers take a long time to learn how to do this and while they are getting to grips with it you can help them manage their behaviour to minimise moodiness and aggression.

THE HOUR RULE

As a **rule of thumb** bear in mind that for every hour spent sitting in front of a screen there should be an hour spent, ideally outdoors, involved in something **physical** (gym, training, swimming, dancing, boxing, riding, walking the dog, fishing).

While indoor activities – reading, cooking, listening to music, acting, drawing/painting and being **creative** – are also good ways of luring your teen away from their console.

Getting engrossed in something should also have the added **benefit** of reducing the need to touch base with the mobile phone.

Positives and negatives

There is a lot of contradictory and confusing information around on the positive and negative effects of gaming. On the one hand we are told that children who game have good reactions and capacities for observation. But that in itself is not enough. In order to develop the analytical capacity in the brain, various parts of the brain need to work in synergy. Gaming reroutes brain traffic away from the process of attending, reflecting and then deciding on a course of action so the child does not spend time processing, learning and remembering what they are doing or playing. Eventually the unused pathways of reflecting and weighing things up will gather dust. Try and moderate these effects of gaming by getting your child involved in activities where they have to concentrate, plan, construct, problem solve and so forth.

Gaming also affects levels of accountability. In the game world, what you do (even if it is dishonourable) does not affect real people and if you don't like the score, you can start again. In terms of teaching morality and conscience, gaming is a non-starter as cheating means you do better.

Try and play plenty of games as a family (e.g. golf, cricket, tennis, volleyball, badminton, races, Monopoly, Scrabble, cards) and play fair. Don't allow even small manipulations of the results or let things go in order to bolster a teenager because they are feeling a little down. Winning feels really good when it follows disappointment and when it is honestly achieved.

Gaming is also inevitably isolating, resulting in fewer real friendships and for many teenagers, becomes addictive. Gaming into the night leads to sleep deprivation, which further compounds the post-gaming exhaustion slump. Keep an eye out for signs of unnatural tiredness and impose limits on access to computers in bedrooms.

Another troubling element is the high level of explicit sexual content in some games. Playing these in the early years (aged eight or nine) starts to normalise the pornographic element. Be vigilant to this and check out which age-inappropriate games are in your house and find out what your children are playing when they are elsewhere. Be frank in your discussions about the kinds of depicted attitudes and behaviour you feel are unacceptable.

Games involving violence or killing have some subliminal influence on the development of real-life attitudes, especially in young boys. Many games involve killing in order to win, which normalises violence, injury and death and desensitises children to these things. Conscience, empathy and morality are all casualties of too much gaming.

Ask your child what games they are playing. Get them to describe them to you in detail. Check out their thought process/beliefs/practices/values around the rules/aims of the game and how this tallies up with the real world. Let them air their views on violence, injury and death. Your opinions will help them to tap into their reflection/feeling zones in their brains.

Smartphones

Try and keep phones out of bedrooms overnight and don't leave them on charge on the bedside table as they interfere with the brain's sleep pattern. Adequate sleep plays an important part in alertness and mood during the day and it also consolidates the day's learning. Teenagers need at least nine hours' uninterrupted sleep per night and not many are getting this. This results in mood dips and some teens can even slip into depression from persistently disturbed sleep.

While your child is young encourage them to get into good habits while also reducing dependency levels. Have a mobile phone park-up, say in the kitchen, where phones can be left and recharged. Apart from health reasons, this also minimises sleep disturbance and the subconscious need to check for messages in the middle of the night. You can also help them to get into the habit of not permanently checking every instant message during the day and enabling them to enjoy interruption-free downtime, which will reduce levels of overdependence and security seeking. Remember, they are watching what you are doing too and learning on the basis of what they see.

Text misunderstandings lead to drama

Teenagers tend to lack the ability to pause and reflect while their emotional brain is in control. The written word carries only 20 per cent of meaning. Eighty per cent of our communication is via voice tone, body language, facial expressions and so forth. Texting increases the tendency for misunderstandings and ambiguity can creep in as words are misread. For example, 'Where are you? You're late,' could be viewed as criticism or concern.

The ability to text fits the instant gratification blueprint. Firing off a text in anger may feel satisfying, but its only purpose may be to add fuel to the confrontational fire. Dealing with 'He said … She said…' via text will only add to the drama.

Being unable to witness the impact their communication has had on its recipient reduces empathy and accountability levels. Help your child to realise that their behaviour and actions do impact others by giving them feedback. If their texts to you seem blunt, hurtful or rude, tell them. You will be helping to develop their social skills.

Banter or bullying?

Problems can quickly develop over the boundaries between fun/teasing/banter/bullying/abuse between young people. Text speak can appear to be quite harsh. Some days your teenager's emotional terrain may read a communication with another person as funny, but the same thing on another day may feel like bullying. If your child keeps getting into hot water with their friends, encourage them to read their texts out loud and wait before they send them, giving them time to check whether there is any potential for misunderstanding.

Relationship damage

The instant gratification element of communicating via text means that children don't develop the art of social conversation – talking, waiting your turn, listening to and being interested in the views of others, responding and building rapport. If your child has a tendency to be on 'send' and butt in while you're talking, help build their awareness and tell them that it is rude to start to talk before someone else has finished their sentence. In effect, you are helping them to be on 'receive' and 'send' at the same time. Conversation is an art and it builds relationships. Being able to verbally communicate well is also essential for job interviews.

Television

TV is a bone of contention in many households. The process of watching television reduces dopamine levels and with it levels of motivation and the ability to learn. There are suggestions that long hours in front of the TV might be associated with raised levels of ADHD and ADD (Attention Deficit Disorder), so if your child has a predisposition to learning difficulties it is worth keeping track of their viewing hours and try and increase hobbies and activities instead.

Keep an eye also on the kinds of attitudes being promoted in the programmes they are watching. Are these what you want them to learn? There is a huge choice available on your cable/

satellite so check that your parental controls are adequate and in place.

As you can see, the consequence of allowing your teenager to overindulge in the wide range of screen-based activities is potentially serious. Trying to curtail them is not easy and requires us as parents to be prepared to be unpopular, to put on our flak jackets and be ready for a detonation. The positive benefit to our children's behaviour and their overall health will pay off in the long term. Get outside and enjoy doing things together.

CHAPTER KEY POINTS

» Technology is responsible for a seismic shift in the attitudes and perceptions of teens and some of the influences are insidious and damaging.

» Some websites are normalising inappropriate and pernicious ideas. Online forums and groups draw in vulnerable teenagers by encouraging and applauding participation in extreme behaviours.

» Minimise isolation by encouraging your child to engage in real face-to-face socialising and physical activity.

» A cyber world operating 24/7 is very pressurised and regular involvement promotes social anxiety. Try to operate a no-screens in bedroom policy at night to ensure better sleep and promote good mood.

» There has been a rise in technology-based addictions, which work on the brain in the same way as alcohol and drugs.

CHAPTER 8
PARENTAL INPUT

If parents want to give their children a gift, the best thing they can do is to teach their children to love challenges, be intrigued by mistakes, enjoy effort, and keep on learning. That way, their children don't have to be slaves of praise. They will have a lifelong way to build and repair their own confidence.
Carol S. Dweck, *Mindset*

This chapter gathers together those parent approaches that are the most helpful during your teenager's transition from child to adult. Whether you are facing normal teenage ups and downs or battling with more serious dramas there are lots of strategies and tools available to you that are proactive and preventative or that can just make things feel better. *Parent reactions and responses are some of the most potent tools we have for positively influencing our children's behaviour.* While the teen brain does its renovations we have a vital window of opportunity to further direct operations.

The way we interact needs to adapt and change in order to support our teenager's growing independence. *In this chapter we are going to look more closely at this changing relationship dynamic, involving behaviour and communication on both sides. See it as being and doing – how you are as a person and what you are doing as a parent in terms of skills.* A good aim is to remember that you are trying to present yourself as a good experience for your child.

Most of us will find that our attention is caught by the things that would be of most benefit to us, so allow your instinct to give you clues as to where to focus your firepower. *The end of this chapter looks at domestic law and order, and gives ideas for how to respond and react to unsettled or downright unacceptable behaviour in order to bring it into line while also reducing the need to punish now that your child is on the cusp of being an adult.*

USING YOUR RELATIONSHIP WITH YOUR TEENAGER TO SET SECURE FOUNDATIONS

When your child was small you were in charge and your role was to be available and to hover over them, protecting and ensuring that they came to no harm. *What your teenager needs now is different and the key shift is that although they still need you, they need you on their terms, not on yours.*

EARLY CONDITIONING AND SOCIALISING

When we are battling with difficult behaviours it is sometimes not easy to remember that behaviour is rolled out for a social purpose and to meet an inner need.[1] Humans are social beings and children are born with an innate need to connect, belong and to feel important, firstly to their parents and then to others. Think back to the early days when your preverbal baby observed and watched you, their parent. Back then they used the relationship they had with you to elicit your love, nurture and attention that ensured their survival. The need for your attention remains the aim of their behaviour – good or bad – even now and as we have seen, if they feel insecure, uncertain, sad or frustrated, the downward spiral of dopamine will push them into their unsettled behaviours.

We will focus here on how our reactions to our teenagers' escapades can be used to subconsciously modify or condition behaviour in order to influence positive change. To do this, we need to begin by looking at anxiety – the root of all unsettled teenage behaviour – but this time from the perspective of the relationship between you and your child.

STEPPING BACK

Loosening the ties in our closest attachments is hard to do and we discussed the biochemical roots of separation anxiety and unsettled behaviour in Chapter 4. The work of John Bowlby (see page 76) focused on the early attachment of babies to their parents, and on their responses to separation.[2] His work helps us understand the inevitable separation process as a child moves through the teenage transition into adulthood. *As a rule of thumb, bear in mind that good early attachments – think calm and settled babies – result in smooth separations and transitions; in other words, less teenage turbulence.*

Cutting the ties and pushing out into the wider world should not be an overwhelmingly anxious experience, but it can be for some. It should be an exciting time for teenagers as they spend more time away from home and experiment with new activities and meet new people. The good feelings and memories acquired from these experiences should raise dopamine, which in turn drives and motivates them to grow up to be confident and successful adults.

But the catch is that this is also a time when the memory files are up in the air (see pages 22–5) and old traumas, behaviour patterns or emotional commotion can re-emerge and scupper proceedings. Overly sensitive biochemical stress levels and raging hormones running alongside also interfere. *What can trigger the trip switch into difficulties and have a long-term impact on your teenager is separation anxiety.*

BEING SEPARATE BUT TOGETHER

When your teenager was a toddler and panic set in – think separation anxiety – they returned to you, their secure base, for reliable comfort and reassurance to soothe their angst. What is happening with your teenager is not that different.

A child whose life up to adolescence has been predictable, consistent and secure with some (but not overwhelming) exposure to difficulties or struggles, will have developed a reasonable threshold of tolerance to disappointment. They should be able to withstand some of the new challenges or setbacks during this period. A child who has encountered much bigger dilemmas when young (changes, moves, loss, grief, confusion, trauma, failure, emotional pain) may also have good tolerance levels but there is the possibility that they may have developed a tendency to overreact and free fall into anxiety and panic at a whiff of drama. Being overly sheltered or protected from making mistakes or taking on challenges could also leave a child struggling to cope when first faced with independent decisions. This may provoke anxiety and stress, throwing up unsettled behaviour in their effort to attract much-needed parental attention that they instinctively know will eventually culminate in the guidance they crave.

To help teenagers to manage independence with minimal anxiety we need to slowly encourage them out on a much longer leash, but at a pace that is tolerable to them. Hard as it is to let them go, try to avoid encouraging reliance on you. This period requires your engagement, courage and patience, both to ride the storm and to celebrate when they manage things on their own. *It requires fine-tuning to strike the right balance between offering support and promoting independence.*

KEEP VALUES AT THE FORE

Values (see page 49) and discussion around **important issues** helps your child to develop their own **conscious understanding** of themselves, which will help them to develop their **autonomy**. These fruitful discussions are sowing the seeds of your child's developing **moral compass and conscience**.

LETTING GO

Letting go of doing things they are capable of doing themselves or advising them on how to do things is a good start. Whenever you can, let go of the controls and let them get on without hovering around with helpful advice, handy tips or micromanagement.

The problem with parachuting in, being too kind or bailing them out, is that children cannot learn strategies or tools to problem solve for themselves. Subconscious patterns of dependency can develop, evidenced by helplessness and powerlessness, effectively disabling your child as they get older.

Your help may be required to pick up the pieces and, hard as it is, try and wait to be asked. You still need to be around and available, but more in the background and ready to come forward when they ask for help. It is important for your teenager to gauge when they need help and to ask for it rather than to expect it or just blunder on when in real difficulty. Offer the support, teaching and encouragement in a constructive rather than a 'that was never going to work' way. They need to learn not only how to bounce back quickly from a setback but also how to manage their anxiety. This process is not helped by parents either doing it for them or hovering with wringing hands and furrowed brows, which are read by the teenager as a vote of no confidence.

Teenagers need to feel encouraged and confident about what lies ahead and feeling their parents' belief in their ability to cope will help them. They are likely to feel varying levels of uncertainty and be quick to pick up on any hints of their incompetence from you. During the teenage period of upheaval and uncertainty it is very anchoring for them to have the sense that someone who is very important has unreservedly got their best interests at heart. You can do this by:

» **Trusting** them enough – to give it a go.
» **Respecting** them – for their efforts and resilience.
» **Expressing** genuine confidence – in their ability to try to find the right path.
» Being **patient** – learning takes time and mistakes are opportunities to develop and learn.

As they get better at managing themselves, their reward from you is that you trust them more, you worry less, they get more freedom and they feel better about themselves. This will leave them feeling more motivated, thoughtful, enthusiastic and appreciative. Try to put worry away as you loosen the reins because in the long term this may fuel resentment and put distance between you and your child.

START WHEN THEY'RE YOUNG

You can make a start on this **letting-go process** with your much younger children. Let them have a go and do age-appropriate things every day (clearing, sorting, picking up and tidying, packing, arranging/remembering kit, minding siblings/pets, cooking, shopping, planning and organising). Any activity once it is well practised becomes an **ingrained habit**. Remind yourself that not doing things for them means you will have less of a commotion later when you expect them to take **complete responsibility** for themselves.

DEALING WITH MISBEHAVIOUR

Think of a misbehaving child as someone who is discouraged, causing them to exhibit yo-yoing moods and confrontational behaviour.[3] This inevitably feeds into an atmosphere between you that is likely to be heavy with unexpressed emotional angst while everyone's brains are hijacked. *If you find yourself in this pattern with your teenager, a key thing to focus on is which particular behaviour keeps catching your eye and think about how you react or discipline this behaviour.*

HOW CAN YOU STOP THE CYCLE?
Your child's negative cycle of behaviour is reinforced and kept rolling by the way you react to it. It may be that your child

CHILD DOES SOMETHING WRONG

ADULT REACTS *with focus on fault and blame*

(Subconscious) **Attention seeking, pattern repeats**

ADULT RESPONDS: punishment/ sanctions or ignores

CHILD BEHAVES/FEELS: **Foolish, angry, moody, defensive, lacks accountability**

CHILD FOCUS: **Injustice, the punisher, or keeps going**

Negative behaviour cycle

is disorganised so you always end up picking up the pieces. Or perhaps your child's pattern is to be rude, disobedient or whinge. This triggers a negative reaction from you, maybe shouting or criticising. This interaction subconsciously mirrors unsettled behaviours back to the child and the situation either escalates into confrontation, or the unsettled behaviours may be replicated and bounced back and forth between you. Either way, an environment of mutual stress and resentment is created, increasing the likelihood of repeating the cycle.

Here's an example of how the wheel might keep turning:

1. The **behaviour** could be: general disrespect, answering back or never helping around the house.
2. The **punishments** so far: you confiscated their phone and now you are about to lock away the Xbox. The next step is to ban television for a week.
3. An **argument** breaks out with a sibling over the remote control. Dad's button is pushed and he reacts with the punishment.
4. The **focus of attention shifts** away from their behaviour to Dad + no television for a week: 'You are the worst parent ever', 'It wasn't just me, she made me', 'It's so unfair you never stop her from watching TV'.
5. Dad may then **feel forced to up the ante** believing that this child needs a **firmer hand**.
6. Emotions are **hijacked** and the atmosphere becomes **threatening, toxic and angry**.
7. The child's **unsettled system** is in full swing and this likely means another bout of **bad behaviour** … and so the **cycle continues** with another misdemeanour in quick succession.

Although it doesn't sound logical, the reason the wheel keeps turning and you both keep repeating the pattern is that the familiarity and predictability of the skirmish offers a child a sort of reassurance and comfort when they are in this emotionally charged anxious state. *Emotionally we derive comfort from whatever pattern is familiar to us, whether that is a good or bad one.*

ACCENTUATE THE POSITIVES

Make sure you pay some **attention** (brief comment, a hug, smile, a thank you) when you have noticed them doing something **positive**. This may **reduce** their need to demand your attention by resorting to the usual negative strategies.

TAKE A CALMER APPROACH

The trouble with these negative behaviour patterns is that they create more trouble, but it is often difficult to decipher where it all started. However, if your child's behaviour or misdemeanours trigger a cascade of worry, eye rolling, clamping down, shame and humiliation, they will avoid turning to you in times of need and be more economical with the truth next time things go wrong. *In order to deal with issues with your teenager calmly, choose how and when to deal with situations and only do so once you feel in control of yourself.* This delayed gratification approach – they sometimes have to learn to wait – will also help to deflate your teenager and train them to calm down more quickly too. Reining in your own reactions changes the quality and texture of your connection in the heat of the moment. Not only will your calmer approach help to reassure them but it will also help reboot your child's negative pattern and reset it on the starting blocks of a different kind of exchange. Keep these things in mind to stop yourself getting unwittingly hooked in.

USE YOUR INTUITION

When you feel that excessive attention is being demanded of you by way of aggression, disobedience, sulking, complaining or being demanding, try and use your intuition. What is your gut telling you about what might have provoked this behaviour? This will help you hone in on what the child might be feeling rather than allowing your button to be pushed by what you are seeing. Think of confrontation and shouting back as putting the wind in your child's sail. *Taking a more intuitive and proactive stance helps you change the course of the interaction.*

LONG-TERM RELATIONSHIP BLUEPRINT

Perhaps you feel railroaded or manipulated on occasion by a demanding daughter or a son who uses sulking or aggression in order to get their own way? It is worth remembering that in order to prevent your child taking these blueprints into other close relationships ('I stamp my foot and eventually I get what I want' or 'I flex my muscles in order to get my own way') we have to change our reactions in order that a different blueprint is rehearsed for the future.

PARENT–CHILD DYNAMIC

A useful way of looking at how to change the dynamic of your relationship is to think of a set of scales. Up until now as a parent you have carried more weight in terms of say so than your child. Now the dynamic needs to slowly move towards becoming a more balanced one. Concerning ourselves with dos and don'ts was part and parcel of parenting a younger child but this needs to play less of a role now.

Teenagers need to know that they will be loved and accepted despite the inevitable ups and downs. There may be times when you are not pleased with their antics, but they need to sense that they are still loved by you, even though their behaviour may not be. It's okay to be angry, but keep your criticism impersonal and levelled at what the child has the potential to change. For example, 'That was a really stupid decision' as opposed to 'You are really stupid'. Try and go for the ball, not the player.

COMMUNICATION STYLES

We need to start modifying our parenting style and Transactional Analysis is a theory that helps us to understand the different layers of how we communicate with our teenagers.[4] Imagine that we all have three different modes of communication:

1. **Parenty**
2. **Adulty**
3. **Childy**

Even more than what we are actually saying (the content), each mode comprises all of our non-verbal communication styles, our voice tone, our body language and our attitudes. These things all leak out when we are talking – the raised eyebrow of sarcasm, the crossed arms of disapproval, the glare of shock.

This is how the modes convey attitudes. Regardless of our age, our Parent attitude stems from concern with safety, control and nurturing ('You should…', 'You must…', 'You

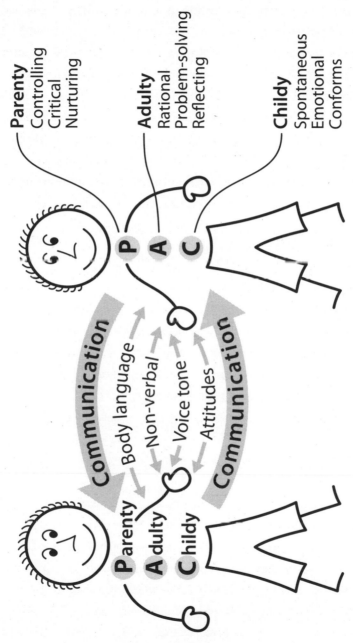

Parenty
Controlling
Critical
Nurturing

Adulty
Rational
Problem-solving
Reflecting

Childy
Spontaneous
Emotional
Conforms

P
A
C

Communication

Communication

Body language
Non-verbal
Voice tone
Attitudes

Parenty
Adulty
Childy

Communication styles

always…'). Our Adult attitude is our rational and objective voice of reason, weighing up, deciding and problem-solving. Our Child attitude is concerned with emotions and spontaneity ('I need…', 'I must…', 'I will…'). When our child was small we were in our Parent mode much of the time and they responded to us from their Child mode. But as they grow up, we will find that using our Parent mode can elicit a rebellious response. *We now need to move across to a more balanced way of communicating with our teenager.* The best way to achieve this is for us to deal with them in Adult mode so that we role-model how it is done.

ROLE-MODELLING

In order that we help create a nice, sociable, pleasure-to-be-with adult, the first thing to bear in mind is **positive role-modelling** (see page 64–5). In other words, by being whatever we would like our teenager to emulate. In Chapters 4–7 we looked at how behaviours and habits get wired up in the brain, but it is worth remembering that things can continue adapting and being conditioned through **observation and imitation** (remember those mirror neurons, page 57). Role-model what you want to see in them.

We mentioned non-verbal detonation in Chapter 2 (see page 26) and how misunderstandings can lead to dramas. Given their hyper-vigilant state, we have to be much more aware of how we are communicating with our teenager because our words will have less meaning than how we deliver them. What teens pick up is our non-verbal emotional state.

Let's say they are back much later than agreed and you greet them with a very terse and tense, 'What time do you call this?' That's you in Parent mode. Their anxiety will be triggered and they are much more likely to give you a rebellious or rude response from their Child mode. This sort of Parent mode (strict, harsh tone and criticising eyes) may unwittingly cause overreactions and create further problems around disciplining (see page 182). Alternatively, we may end up at the other end of the Parent mode spectrum and feel sick with worry about them going out again and staying out late because they may get into trouble. This kind of Parent mode (smothering/overly protective) might elicit problems in the child with dependency and separation.

BEING IN ADULT MODE

If we stayed in our Adult mode in the above situation, we may say something like, 'I feel too cross to discuss this now because this wasn't what we agreed, so let's talk tomorrow and see what we can do to make sure we don't end up in this mess again next time.' Sticking to a clear, calm, straightforward Adult mode of communication is going to help your messages get through and it will help your teenager develop their own Adult way of being and doing.

Take a look at the diagram on the next page. The ideas will help to keep you anchored and more in your Adult mode.

PARENT AIMS:
Emphasis on
REFLECTION;
use opportunity
to help child
UNDERSTAND
and LEARN
(meaningful punishment
if necessary)

PARENT IS DOING:
DISCUSSING limits and giving
WARNINGS; GUIDING, being
FLEXIBLE and NEGOTIATING win/win;
using HUMOUR appropriately

PARENT IS BEING:
CALM (reactions);
CLEAR (values);
FAIR (firm boundaries);
NON-JUDGEMENTAL (attitudes)

Encouraging positive behaviour

HOLD BALANCED DISCUSSIONS

Make sure that discussions are as balanced as possible. This will involve asking questions, allowing reflection and listening to their plans while offering gentle guidance. *Try to adopt a more Adult-to-Adult approach in how you talk.* Be interested rather than inquisitive, chatty rather than lecturing and offer a range of suggestions rather than one directive. This will help them get into the habit of thinking through pros and cons in a supported atmosphere with you. Teenagers are notorious at making hasty and ill-considered decisions so encourage them to reflect on things rather than adopt the shotgun approach.

Try to anticipate thorny issues by having an open, non-judgemental discussion about other people's misdemeanours. So much learning can be done by having a philosophical discussion about teenage issues. Done this way you may be able to remain

THE POWER OF EYE CONTACT

There are few things as powerful as **eye contact** in showing you **care.** This was the primary mechanism you and your baby used to bond, via oxytocin, and it is the quickest way to top up your teenager's **emotional tank,** leaving them calm and reassured. Oxytocin moderates stress levels and promotes a sense of support, comfort and trust with you. Generally, girls love face-to-face chatting so they tend to use eye contact when socialising, but some boys can find eye contact more challenging and intrusive, so chats in the car with occasional looks might work better for them. But bear in mind that gentle momentary glances are just as effective in topping up the tank.

However, eye contact can be misinterpreted by your teenager depending on how you have used it over the years. It can be a **powerful communicator** of disapproval, disgust, anger, frustration and resentment as well as sadness or fear. A good tip is to think of your eyes as being the **window to your soul.** Use them to convey approval ('I'm here, you're great') so they get acclimatised to eye contact being a **nice experience.**

If you are aware that your child does not hold eye contact with you or other adults either easily or for long, which may come across as being self-centred or defensive, introduce this very gradually. This will allow them to build up tolerance levels in order to be able to hold eye contact for longer periods. Good eye contact in a teenager might indicate higher levels of security and confidence, a sort of **comfortable-in-their-own-skin attitude.**

more anchored, objective, empathic and calm thereby providing an atmosphere for your child to understand where you stand (on issues like teenage drinking, for example). Judgement risks turning the discussion into a 'You never liked him/her anyway' event. Resist those terribly tempting phrases like 'I warned you about him/her'.

COMMUNICATION TOP TIPS

We have talked about our non-verbal communication style and here are a few more skills to consider when talking with your teenager. The aim is to help develop the sort of respect and environment that keeps lines of communication open.

LISTEN... BUT ACTIVELY

How often have you experienced someone who is preoccupied but insists they are listening? The reality is that it doesn't feel that way. Listening is not a passive exercise. Active listening involves establishing an environment that encourages talking – hold eye contact, smile, spend time and be together and not be distracted by other things like your phone. *Try and create a climate in which your child might feel secure enough with you and trust your reactions to take the risk of talking to you about what is painful or embarrassing for them.*

ENCOURAGE THEM TO TALK

Talking is the key to change because laying out your stall can help you to see things more clearly and change the meaning that you attach to turbulent feelings. Although it isn't easy to encourage, especially in teenage boys, it is worth doing because translating an inner emotional experience into words is what allows us to move from seeing it subjectively to being able to get some clarity on it. This can often result in a change of feeling and attitude towards that issue and this is in part why counselling works.

Being able to reflect and think about past experiences and current dilemmas and to discuss the potential consequences of decisions not only helps to inform the present, but it is also banked for future problem-solving situations. If you can help your teenager by creating this sort of environment their young brain is being assisted to learn how to control its impulsive knee-jerk reactions as well. If you have a thorny issue you wish to raise, start by talking about other things and not necessarily the issue. Alternatively, if you have a child who does not find talking easy, get the wheels of discussion oiled by getting them to talk about anything they feel strongly about. This gets them used to their own voice and used to being heard.

GUIDING NOT LECTURING

Infuriating as it is, lecturing rarely works. It would be so much easier if we could just lecture our children on the pros and cons of something and instantly achieve a change in their behaviour. But unfortunately it doesn't work that way and when we encounter something that doesn't strike a chord, the information literally does pass in one ear and out of the other.

So what does this mean for our relationship with our teenagers? Let's take the teenage drinking example. Wading in with your alcohol talk is not likely to do the trick. If you are lucky and things are going well, your teenager may agree with you, but your healthier option is unlikely to be uppermost in their minds as they put their hand out for their fourth triple vodka Red Bull.

We have to get more creative in our guidance and discussions in order to kick-start that sort of light-bulb moment!

Teenagers can have a tendency to live in a fantasy world. 'Health issues, ageing, having accidents – they won't happen to me!' Using some real-life stories can work well to open up reflective discussion, and fear is an effective wake-up call too. If you detect that they have registered something during the chat, try and avoid the temptation of driving the point home because this may backfire if they feel directed by you. The hardest thing to do is to gauge when you have said enough and to stop, but doing so will avoid them defying you because your lecture has annoyed them. Instead leave it to slowly sink in so that the seed is sown and they can reflect on it themselves. When they come up with a decision along the lines of what you were hinting at in your conversation, resist the temptation to claim it as your idea!

USE HUMOUR

Don't forget that humour is a good way to diffuse tense situations, provided it is not misread by your teenager as laughing at them. If they sense this, they read it as humiliation. Also make sure that your mirth does not come over as 'this is trivial and really doesn't matter'. If you consider that your child dabbling with marijuana at 16 or getting very drunk at 14 is serious, then don't be overheard laughing it off with your friends.

THE IMPORTANCE OF BOUNDARIES

An adult without boundaries is stuck with a drive to have more, more, more. Although their unbridled lack of self-control may seem like fun in the early years, someone without a brake pedal cannot gauge when to change gear, or stop, and that can be scary when they are let loose in temptation alley. The personality that emerges lacks self-governance, does not know where the limit is and at worst has no moral compass to help distinguish right from wrong. They just keep going, getting themselves into hot water, but genuinely believing it's never their fault.

Don't confuse boundaries with control. *Imposing firm limits teaches resilience, which is the cornerstone of all flourishing relationships.* The way to do it is to not be afraid of allowing rupture within your relationship with your teenager. If you say no to something then the child learns how to tolerate disappointment, frustration, accept limits and how to bounce back. The key is how to manage the repair of your relationship without your child free-falling into feelings of resentment and revenge and manipulating a change of decision on your part. Parents have to be prepared to be unpopular. The long-term benefit is that your relationship will improve and your child will be more resilient and able to ride the storms of ups and downs.

FLEXIBILITY WITHOUT SURRENDER

But we also need to be flexible during the period that they are growing up and realise that what was an appropriate boundary for an 11-year-old will need to be adapted for an 18-year-old.

Negotiation should not be seen as capitulation. A good tip is to steal their thunder and get ahead of the game by noticing what might need to change and initiate discussion and renegotiate something that works for both of you. Don't wait until you are railroaded into submission – 'Everyone else is allowed to…', 'Nobody else's parents ever…'. The result of feeling as if you have capitulated and been beaten is a false feeling of power in your child, who feels as if they have won so they learn to use this tactic again next time. But subconsciously, they are also left feeling uncertain and anxious about who is actually in charge.

Inflexibility – for example keeping control, fussing, lecturing, watching for every mistake, being rigid about boundaries – will only work for as long as your child is under your roof. It will also teach your child to up the ante in order to get their own way. Aim to set up the sort of relationship now where they are encouraged to talk to you and hear your views, then this will continue long after they have left the nest.

GOOD, FIRM DISCIPLINING

Where you can establish a relationship that infuses your teenager with the will to cooperate with you, you are already well on the way to avoiding having to punish at all. To get to this point, you will have kept closely to your values, been largely calm and maintained the moral high ground (without being sanctimonious) when dealing with thorny issues. In a nutshell, you will have created an atmosphere where your child does not wish or need to overstep the mark too often because they respect you.

ENCOURAGING REFLECTION ABOUT MISDEMEANOURS
Think of bad behaviour as a poor effort at communicating and our job is to find out what the child is actually trying to say. This is not to suggest that we should be laissez-faire and let our children get

away with bad behaviour, but it is to say that once the crime has been committed, wait until both you and they are calm and have full access to Brain 3 before tackling the situation. Then create the right climate by holding composed discussions and asking questions with the purpose of getting the child to think things through, be accountable and not do the same thing again.

PUNISHMENTS THAT FIT THE CRIME

Punishments need very careful management. They need to be meted out in ways that trigger enough shame in your child that they feel bad/embarrassed/ashamed about what they have done, but not so much that the brain gets hijacked, resulting in overwhelming humiliation and a defensive shutdown.

There are times, however, when you need to take the next step and punish. *Make sure any punishment you dole out is meaningful and fits the crime.* You have probably got the right balance if you think your child thinks 'Fair dos, I got it wrong and I am paying this price'.

It is important to make sure that the sanction does not end up punishing you (trying to uphold no television for the week) or make you look foolish (one child can't watch television but the other can, or you can't contact your child for pickups because you have confiscated their phone). Think about getting them to do something useful like weeding the garden or tidying the shed. This will also give you an opportunity to thank them for their help while reminding them why they ended up doing this task in the first instance.

If your disciplining procedures (either via reflection or punishment) are working, you should have a sense that your child bounces back, that they learn from the misdemeanour, that they are discouraged to reoffend and are better equipped to take responsibility for future decisions. And the climate you have created means, when the dust has settled, they are still warm and affectionate to you.

THREATS AND BRIBES

There is a fine line between extrinsic motivation, where there is an actual physical reward or bribe (or threats of punishment) for inducing good behaviour and intrinsic motivation where your child's natural wish to please will drive them to cooperate because their reward is a sense of belonging and feeling good. Bribing is just like any other addictive habit. The more you use it, the more you will need to do next time to get their compliance.

The inbuilt human desire to socialise and to feel good by connecting with others is what makes your teenager pull out all the stops, for instance for some teachers/subjects at school, while for others they slope off to make paper darts at the back of the class. The more we as parents can be aware of how we are being and what we are doing, the more we will be able to generate cooperation.

DRIP-FEED FEEL-GOOD NOURISHMENT

Think of yourself as forming a **new relationship** with your **emerging teenager** who is in many ways becoming a new adult person. This emerging relationship will thrive if it is **balanced and collaborative** and can withstand the hurly-burly of adolescence. The parental long-term agenda – the **finest legacy** you can bestow – is that your child feels **valued, capable and encouraged** and they are equipped with a firm sense of what is **okay and what is not**.

EXPERIENCING SCHOOL LIFE

School is part and parcel of your teenager's life and is one of their social stamping grounds. Experience-based learning happens through being part of a group and it challenges thoughts, beliefs and attitudes. This is how our child will build their self-awareness. Giving children space to develop their own independence is an important part of the later stages of school life. Teenagers need to become socially and emotionally independent and branch out into a wider social network.

DAY SCHOOL

Under the watchful eye of their parents, day school pupils may find it hard to carve out independent space. You may struggle with their new demands for a freer rein after school. This may leave you feeling as if you have no means of checking up on what they are doing.

BOARDING SCHOOL

Children at boarding school have to become more independent more quickly as ties to home are cut and they are required to cope with experiences without family support.

Homesickness is in fact separation anxiety (see page 76), so if your child is struggling to pick up the reins of independence they may need your encouragement to do so. Take care that none of your sadness or anxiety leaks out through your voice as this may compound their lack of confidence.

A child at boarding school may need an outlet, on occasion, to express their feelings when things go wrong. One end of the spectrum is the development of a stiff upper lip, where a child learns how to cope with all their problems on their own because they feel there is no help available. The other end of the spectrum is that your child becomes dependent on offloading on to you and is constantly in phone contact. Ideally, over time, they need to learn to manage themselves independently of you.

BULLYING

School should be an experience that encourages confidence, respect and self-governance. However, where a group of people are in close quarters on a regular basis there is a potential for outbreaks of unacceptable behaviour – particularly if the group is made up of overemotional and hormonally charged teenagers. There is a wealth of information offering support about bullying online (see page 225). It is worth thinking about how parents and family can help too.

> » Help your child to understand that they **cannot control someone else's behaviour**, but they can control their **responses and reactions** to that person. This is a good first step towards **empowerment**.
>
> » Tell the child to use their **invisible shield** (see page 201) and decide to no longer allow this person's behaviour to drag them down. This a **good mindset** for them to adopt.
>
> » Encourage your child to **distract themselves** by using any of the healthy coping strategies (see pages 102–4). This will help **boost their morale**.
>
> » Tempting as it is to ring school – if this is where the unacceptable behaviour started – **check** this with your teenager first. Sometimes the mere idea that you might complain is enough for a child to realise that they can **sort it out for themselves**.

» Sometimes being rescued by a parent – or an older sibling – **risks** the child being singled out and further **compounds the troubles**.

» Spending time in **supportive discussion** with you around empowering your child to seek out ways to manage the problem for themselves can help **boost resilience**, particularly if you can encourage a **'Yes I can'** attitude to resolving it.

DEALING WITH EXAM STRESS

We have talked about negative mindsets and you may find one creeps into your family in the run-up to important exams. You may start to hear sweeping statements like 'I am going to fail', 'What's the point?', 'I'm going to give up' or observe lethargic body language that communicates a similar message.

Your child's working mind is evidenced by their mindset (see page 43) and it runs like an inner script (see pages 197–8 for more on this). If consistent negative dialogue creeps in it will set the scene. A blip around exam time is understandable even if your child is normally reasonably optimistic. Even so, it is worth encouraging your child to spend less brain time worrying about something that might not happen and more time developing good mental habits and harnessing energy in planning a successful outcome. 'I can't' needs to be transformed into 'I might try to…'.

To help your teenager do this spend time with them compiling a doable revision schedule, think about what help is needed, identify who might be able to help, and map out realistic and achievable goals. Try to strike the right balance between being helpful and encouraging dependence and helplessness. This is reinforced by parents doing too much – 'Let me help you with your revision'. But this may result in your child offloading the blame on to you – 'If you had helped me more, I could have done better'.

Try to avoid both a 'snap out of it' approach (which raises stress chemicals) and false jollity – 'I'm sure you will be fine, you're bound to pass', neither will result in the smooth running of Brain 3.

CHAPTER KEY POINTS

» Try to move your relationship dynamic from managing your child to letting them get on with things. Strike the right balance between offering support and promoting independence.

» Be aware of how you are – voice tone, attitude, body language, facial expression, eye contact – because teens are very sensitive to this. Move to an Adult-to-Adult mode of communicating.

» Bad behaviour is a poor effort at communicating an emotional need. Use your intuition to identify the need and provide reassurance.

» Think about what you are doing and role-modelling in response to negative behaviour cycles.

» Boundaries, boundaries, boundaries. But don't confuse them with exercising control or power.

» Use firm, but not harsh, discipline and think carefully about punishment.

» Behaviour is on a spectrum. Like a language it takes practice and time to develop.

CHAPTER 9
IN CONCLUSION
– THE FAMILY MELTING POT

I have come to a … conclusion that … my personal approach creates the climate. It is my daily mood that makes the weather … I possess tremendous power to make a child's life miserable or joyous. I can be a tool of torture or an instrument of inspiration, I can humiliate or humor, hurt or heal. In all situations, it is my response that decides whether a crisis is escalated or de-escalated.
Haim G. Ginott, *Teacher and Child*

HOW TO USE FAMILY LIFE TO GIVE YOUR CHILDREN THE WINGS TO FLY

Family life is where so much learning and discovery happens for our children – about themselves, how they respond and operate, about others and about how to be part of a group. Knowing who they are and what drives them is a slow and important realisation. When they know this and they live in a way that accords with what really matters to them, they will find contentment.[1] The eminent psychologist Carl Rogers called this process of discovery 'self actualisation' and argued that it was a vital cornerstone to achieving self-esteem. The hurly-burly of family life is a crucial place to help them discover and work this out and test it against the other relationships at home. In addition, so much of a child's time is spent in the crucible of the family that what happens here – the atmosphere and the interactions – has a huge impact.

Relationship dynamics between the different people – parents, siblings and step-relatives – can be complicated and knowing, for instance, how the differences between sons and daughters play out in the family helps us handle these dynamics better and achieve a more stable home environment. *This chapter is going to look at family life and key relationships at home so we can use these to the best advantage.*

The atmosphere at home matters. Life in the family is fertile learning ground. You are setting the tone in your home. If the family melting pot is flavoured with irritation, confrontation, defeatism, defensiveness, power struggles, withdrawal, inconsistency or shouting, then this becomes your child's hallmark and legacy. *What we need is for our young adult to emerge out of this melting pot with a solid sense of self and a confidence to tackle what lies ahead.*

CREATING A SAFE HAVEN

All families will have their own particular culture and norms that hold them together as a group. These provide our children with feelings of safety and security. In order to achieve this, what goes on inside our four walls at home needs to be consistent and predictable. We all learn more through active experience and our family relationships provide rich opportunities to learn through active doing.

TURN UP THE CENTRAL HEATING

For children to develop the ability to connect with others and build warm relationships they need to have experienced this themselves. Home is the perfect place to learn this so make sure that your house feels warm, welcoming and optimistic. Take time to enjoy being with the family, talking and joking (remember the power of humour to feel good) and showing them affection. Down tools – even if only briefly – when anyone walks in, especially those close to you, and look pleased to see them. You can't teach warmth, but you can demonstrate how it is done. If your child is upset, make sure you show genuine concern and compassion. When things go wrong, avoid grudges, sort problems out in a way that allows you to move on, forgiving and forgetting. Problems creep in when we are not candid and things remain unsaid, so learning how to deal with misunderstandings or disagreements is a crucial life skill for our teenagers.

Family time is a casualty of today's busy technology-dominated world and it's often hard to carve out time for you as a group. Try and prioritise this as doing things as a family – going for a walk, playing a game, cooking or even reading together in the same room – reiterates your connection as a unit. It also demonstrates to your child that they are important enough to you to find space and time for. They will see you looking enthusiastic, relaxed and getting the work/play balance right and they will absorb how to do this too.

STICK TO ROUTINES AND RITUALS

Mealtimes are a golden opportunity for relaxing and being together as well as providing consistent routines. Apart from it teaching your children basic social skills, such as talking, listening and showing genuine interest in what other people have to say, it is also a way to open up general discussions and for you to check out views, opinions and current attitudes. You will have a chance to put in your penny's worth on where you stand, without it seeming like a lecture. Imposing a no-mobile zone really helps to prevent constant interruptions and distractions.

Traditions make family life feel even safer so where a child can rely on the predictable and consistent – 'We always have Sunday lunch' – it gives them a sense of a secure anchor.

Birthdays and celebrations provide another opportunity for predictability and something to look forward to. Perhaps you always go out for birthdays, open Christmas presents by the tree or have a favourite meal on the last night of a holiday. Despite the increasing need for parents to provide activities, outings and entertainment for the family, sometimes the simple things – all having candlelit supper together – can feel just as rewarding.

HAVING PETS

Pets are a great addition to the household and can provide **distraction and comfort** when teenagers are stressed or having a difficult time. Looking after them helps children **develop empathy** by attending to someone else's needs before their own. **Taking responsibility** for feeding or cleaning up the kennel/cage/stable is a good routine that **builds cooperation and requires consistency.** Many pets also provide an excuse for children to get **outdoors and take some exercise.**

THE DYNAMICS OF FAMILY RELATIONSHIPS

Experiencing the ups and downs of family life in a secure setting provides the ideal platform for children to develop solid friendships with siblings and the confidence to have intimate, loving relationships as adults.

Your family life will have a certain rhythm and changes can upset the applecart when new people are introduced into the dynamic so be vigilant to this. These can be a new partner for a divorced or separated parent, the arrival of step-siblings or your children's own partners as they grow up, for example.

BEING A COUPLE

Parents or couples living in close quarters can role-model two important qualities to the family. *The first is respect.* Children can imbibe how to interact with those close to them in a reasonable and respectful way. *The second is cooperation.* Where the adults in the household are willingly helping each other out and offering support they are demonstrating how to work as a team. It is worth remembering that it is not so much what we are saying to each other, but how it is said that gets results. However, being cooperative loses its appeal if there is no benefit, so showing gratitude and appreciation, when appropriate, helps to develop the habit.

Remind yourself that your child is watching the texture of the relationship between parents or adults in the household and subconsciously taking in how to successfully negotiate close relationships themselves. For instance, what happens when things go wrong? Are emotions bottled up until they are no longer manageable? Unresolved conflicts brushed under the carpet? Or if they are tackled, how are they tackled? If our children see a pattern of not communicating, this may re-emerge later in their lives. Try and keep the door open. *Keep talking, keep arguing, keep resolving, keep apologising, keep allowing mistakes, keep forgiving, keep loving.*

MANAGING DIVORCE

Parents sometimes worry about the impact of divorce on their child but what really matters is how the discord is handled. Toxic relationships, evidenced by what is not being said between two people, arguments that happen behind closed doors but are overheard, point-scoring comments or a whispering campaign to get others to take sides are very confusing blueprints for children to imbibe, causing anxiety, unsettled behaviour and possible trips to temptation alley. Often a child will feel guilty about how they might have contributed to the relationship decline, believing that they could have saved things. With the emotional teenage brain having a tendency to overreact, coupled with black-and-white (and often entirely illogical) thinking (e.g. 'This is all my fault', 'If I hadn't caused trouble at school after GCSEs my parents might still be okay'), it is important that parents offer straightforward openness and clarity wherever possible. This will go a long way to soothing your child's anxiety.

What can be maintained during divorce is the unique and loving relationship you have with your child. What will also help is for them to know that each parent continues to love them and that any acrimony between parents is separate and does not spill over into the parent–child relationship and family life. Remember that feeling loved and secure comes from the attitudes we talked about above: the warmth of what we are expressing rather than saying – a soothing voice, reassuring eye contact, interest in the child and time spent together. Simply being told they are loved is not enough.

SEEK SUPPORT

It is especially important during break-ups and divorce that parents **look after themselves.** Make sure you get plenty of **support and find a safe space** (ideally counselling) in which to **vent your emotions** so that you do not end up inadvertently confiding in your child by speaking disparagingly about your ex-partner. During the teenage years it is especially important for children to continue to **respect both of their parents.**

SIBLINGS

Sibling relationships (including with stepfamilies) provide a good practice ground for social and emotional development. Siblings will argue and compete and get really upset with each other. However, like any other relationship, they will be stronger if they can learn how to withstand the ruptures and make the necessary repairs. If step-siblings are being introduced into their life this will be an emotionally complex time for everyone. Resentment and jealousy can creep in, but even-handed reassurance and fair treatment among all the children will go some way to alleviating this.

Getting on with siblings is about learning the art of rubbing along with others through good and bad times. If a damaging relationship is developing in your family it is worth trying to rectify and rebalance the dynamics and not leave it to fester. The sorts of things we as parents can help them with are:

» **Sorting out disagreements** – gather them together and allow each side to have their say in order to find a way forward, as opposed to letting them use you as the go-between.
» **Forgiveness** – get them to draw a line under it and genuinely move on without resentment, making sure that you don't blame anyone either.
» **Toleration** – improve levels of consideration for others living in close quarters. This is helped by listening to the impact of your actions on others and aiming to modify own behaviour.
» **Empathy** – is improved when everyone offers support to a family member when it is needed.
» **Self-control** – learning to toe the line even when they vehemently disagree and developing the art of discussion.

BOYFRIENDS AND GIRLFRIENDS

Just before boyfriends/girlfriends start appearing on the horizon, it is worth setting out the boundaries and explaining why you have whatever rules you have in your house. The rest of the family will replicate whatever happens with your eldest child, so tread cautiously. Check out your teenager's sexual attitudes too. We can help them to think through and formulate this new relationship so that it accords with their values and help ensure that they are not feeling pressured to behave in ways that might corrode their self-respect.

The regular presence in your home of your teenager's partner, and their closeness to your child, may disturb the other relationships temporarily, so being prepared for this is helpful. Other siblings may feel pushed out of the hallowed circle of the couple or may feel resentful about the relationship. How they get on with the new person will also have a bearing. We can help to sand off some of these rough edges by modelling how to be relaxed, warm, inclusive and welcoming.

LEARNING ABOUT WHO THEY ARE

Knowing who they are is not easy as children develop into adults and it can take time – through trial and error for them to work out what feels comfortable and instinctively right for them. A child can gather an accurate perception of themselves via feedback from close relationships at home. *Self-esteem is how we perceive ourselves to be (self-confidence is rated on doing)*. Ideally we need our child to be realistic and have neither an inflated sense of who they are nor a self-deprecating one. Alongside this they need to be able to accurately assess their strengths and weaknesses, and seeing these against those of their siblings helps them to get a clearer picture. However, because the teenage brain has a tendency to misinterpret attitudes and jump to negative conclusions – 'They have never liked me', 'She thinks I am rubbish' – this can steer self-esteem off course. We can help by gently challenging any persistent negative language in order to get them back on track.

Falling into roles can also nudge our children into different ways of being because their role in the family will be defined by everyone else's views on them. Expectations will arise out of these: 'He is always the family joker', 'She is the clever one', 'He's the baby of the family'. Very quickly our children will end up playing the part. Our job is to be vigilant to this and to prevent very specific roles and identities being constructed, particularly if they are not an accurate representation of our child. Negative beliefs can have a slow-burn effect and subconsciously drive a child to develop a negative inner script. If this happens, rather like negative beliefs around failing exams, they will start to live life according to their script.[2]

Based on what we know about the teenage brain and underlying emotional needs, we have listed below in the first column a few goals for parents to try to aim for as part of the family approach. We have highlighted in the central column the sorts of comments that, if used, would be unhelpful. The last column shows you some of the possible negative outcomes resulting from these statements.

TIPS FOR PARENTS

Parent Goal	Avoid comments such as	Likely negative outcome
Resist inter-family comparisons and allow children to be different and to develop at their own pace	'I am worried about your work attitude. Jessica is younger than you but she already seems to be further ahead. Try taking a leaf out of her book!'	» Comparisons between siblings are a confusing way of giving feedback and establish an atmosphere of unhealthy competition where children are constantly vying for your attention and that extra brownie point » The emotional fallout is jealousy, long-term resentment and potential warfare

Parent Goal	Avoid comments such as	Likely negative outcome
Modify criticism and judgement	'I think you have got a screw loose, you do some ridiculous things and I'm beginning to wonder about where you are heading.'	» Comments like this compound anxiety and stress in the child
Adopt an attitude where mistakes are seen as an opportunity to grow and learn	'You're an idiot, yet again you didn't think this one through and you are not going to get away with it.'	» Being draconian about trying things out runs the risk of upping the ante or the child becoming reluctant to attempt things in the future
Help the decision-making process	'Come on, you really must get on with it and decide one way or the other.' 'Well you have obviously not really thought this one through. Even I can see where things are going to go wrong.'	» Not investing time in discussion means children are not able to develop a more objective standpoint » Impatience stifles creativity and their ability to come up with their own ideas » Criticism and judgement increase levels of stress and reduce levels of motivation

Parent Goal	Avoid comments such as	Likely negative outcome
Reduce fear and improve confidence	'Why do you never want to give things a go? You're so stubborn!'	» This may compound an already risk-averse mindset where they are fearful of moving out of their comfort zone » An unadventurous mindset harbouring feelings of powerlessness and helplessness
If it's flaky, tell them, so they realise that their behaviour can come across as unreliable or untrustworthy	'I thought you said that you were going to make that telephone call yesterday? It's a familiar story with you, you always say you are going to do things, but you never do.'	» Indecision is rooted in uncertainty and fear. Getting irritated and judgemental about it can further prolong avoidance and prevarication

MUM AND DAD, SON AND DAUGHTER

Their closest relationships are with you, their parents, and teenagers scrutinise the texture of their communication with you with a subconscious aim of basing their own behaviour on what they see. *There are some distinctive shades to the different relationships.*

MUM'S RELATIONSHIP WITH DAUGHTER

Girls are especially sensitive to the atmosphere around them and will be watching interactions between immediate family members much more closely once hitting puberty. Keep an eye out for what is going on at home. If you are uneasy about what your teenage daughter is imbibing via your own situation, siblings, boyfriend/girlfriend or close friends try to have a clear and un-loaded chat with her. Your relationship needs to become more Adult-to-Adult (see pages 172–8) and not over-nurturing or protecting (see pages 164–7) while ties need to be cut (see page 163–4).

During this transition it is important for her to get the line right between 'We are so close, I tell my mother everything' and 'I would never dream of telling my mother anything'. However, girls will feel more emotionally in control if you give them opportunities to talk things through with you. Help them learn to protect themselves from life's arrows by helping them to work out what is right for them and what is not – in other words, establishing their own boundaries (see page 165). Be pleased if they are asserting their quest for independence and allow arguments to happen in a non-confrontational way.

» Help your daughter develop some **emotional control** by telling her to imagine that she has an **invisible shield** that can reject the bad things but lets good things in.

» **Encourage** her to talk to you, but not to give you chapter and verse. This will help her to understand **limits** in her own close relationships.

» Encourage discussions around her **developing opinions and decision-making**. If you feel she is heading in the wrong direction over something, urge her to think about **other plans** too.

» When the time is right, give her the **confidence** to have a close relationship.

» **Role-model** how to have a **good argument** by first listening to her and checking your understanding, then by allowing her to assert her needs and views without letting it become **confrontational**.

» Remember that anger tends to turn **inwards** in women and may express itself as **sadness**, so female hurt or sadness may be **masking anger**.

» **Eye contact** (see page 177) is especially important to girls because it helps them feel **connected** when they are talking about important things.

MUM'S RELATIONSHIP WITH SON

As mothers, we can feel shut out and hurt when our teenage sons transform overnight and suddenly appear unable to discuss or express any form of emotion. To add insult to injury, they sometimes also develop a tendency to overreact towards our emotion with fight/aggression or flight/exiting stage left. All of this emotional fog will clear once our son's emotional toleration levels have found their equilibrium, so we need to hang on and be patient. What is happening is that sons need to get some emotional distance from mum, while their focus is on learning how to become a man. But they also need to know that the closeness is still available, so it can be a difficult balance to strike.

Remind yourself that your interactions will help keep them emotionally grounded long term. In order to smooth out this turbulent period and help get things on an even keel really try and avoid a nagging/shouting routine. Try acting dumb to check out plans: 'Have you had any thoughts about...?', as opposed to 'Don't do...'. Not only can you then help your son to engage Brain 3 and link his actions to consequences, but you can then congratulate him on his plan, which improves his confidence. Admire the good male qualities he is developing so he gets a sense that he is going in the right direction.

» Try to **contain the tears** and **resist nagging** as both might evoke aggression or a swift exit.
» **One request** at a time for boys. They find it harder than girls to multitask, so overloading them runs the risk of **triggering defiance or rudeness**.
» Try not to **misread** their inability to articulate as hostility.
» Try to keep lines of **communication calm** so Brain 2 doesn't hijack proceedings.
» **Sadness** in men is more likely to be **displayed as anger**, so stay attuned to what might be going on behind the scenes.
» Allow opportunities to **talk**. Boys respond better to **conversations** that take place **while doing something else**, e.g. walking, driving, cooking.
» Talk about what you believe girls might **expect from boyfriends** so your son can form his own views.
» Keep **talking through** plans, ideas, implications, while the actions/consequence, brain link is still unstable. Don't force decisions.
» Admire him, but **don't** put him on a pedestal.
» **Don't stop** the physical contact altogether but do it **differently** – a quick hug or goodnight kiss rather than an emotional goodbye in front of his friends. Take the lead from him.
» Bear in mind that if he has to fight for his **much-needed** emotional distance from you, he is more likely to turn to more **hurtful behaviours** to do this.

DAD'S RELATIONSHIP WITH DAUGHTER

Loosening the ties between fathers and daughters can be as painful as mothers and sons. Sometimes dads find their little girl turning into a woman a difficult transition and working out how to respond to her can take time. Partners appearing on the scene add to the change, but it's good news if she can hold down a healthy, long-term relationship. In order that she can be comfortable with men, she needs to feel what it is like to be respected, admired and comfortable around you. You may even have to have the dreaded sex and pornography talk if mum is not around. It will help her to hear the healthy male perspective on sex because it will help her set her limits.

Dad also needs to be ready to face the extremes of girly emotions. Although you can help stabilise things through your more logical approach, remember that your logic can be infuriating for her when she is in meltdown mode. So gauge it carefully – a little at a time. Your measured reactions will also help her realise that men respond to strident female emotions differently to women and that doesn't mean they don't care.

Sometimes you will need to say no and girls react well to the clear-cut male voice of authority. Aim for your new Adult-to-Adult communication style to include genuine warmth and connection so that it carries mutual respect.

> » Prepare yourself for **disappointment** when she falls in love with someone else.
> » Be **careful** how you view your daughter. Being a princess and having daddy wrapped – dewy-eyed and besotted – around her little finger sets a **tough yardstick** for her future partner.
> » While she is growing into a woman, **listen** to her

opinions, so she has experience of being **respected** and taken **seriously**.

» Don't be afraid to **lay down the law** every now and then. It will **teach** her to live within **limits**.

» If she needs to talk to you on an emotional level, be ready to **listen** and **respond calmly and logically**, but take care that your male style is not misread as cold and uncaring.

DAD'S RELATIONSHIP WITH SON

Boys cut the metaphorical apron strings from mum at puberty and turn their attention to dad or other male figures to emulate. The presence of other important men is vital at this stage (stepfather, brother, grandfather, uncle, teacher) and they will have a profound influence on your son, so try to make sure that they embody the sorts of attitudes that you would like your son to experience.

Managing the move from Parent mode to a relationship in Adult mode (see pages 172–8) can be complicated. As your son grows up, the relationship can move into skirmishes around rivalry, control and teaching them a thing or two. Dad needs to try and stay out of this power play and create a respectful relationship by balancing being authoritative whilst promoting healthy competition.

Remember what we said about shame being toxic. Teenage boys can have a tendency to overreact to failure, harsh discipline or ridicule with defensive or disrespectful behaviours. Bad behaviour will put his head above the parapet, resulting in more trouble around the corner.

Teenage boys need to learn how to connect at an emotional level and dad is the person they are least likely to confide their true feelings to. Tough as it is, dad needs to start trying to build his son's capacity to do so. Meaningful or spontaneous but short discussions, listening, engaging in eye contact and asking questions provides an environment to sound out developing opinions or ideas. Your approval or praise is invaluable and boys need it to help them establish a sense of competence and confidence in their abilities.

Dad needs to make sure that he is role-modelling what he wants his son to turn out like.

» Engage in **side-by-side activities** that take time. Boys can take **hours to open up**, so a game of golf, a long walk or a car journey might provide an **opportunity to talk**.

» Discuss your **own emotions** where appropriate so that they see that it is **okay** to have an **emotional world**.

» If your son gets emotional it may evoke shame or embarrassment. Make sure you are **ready to accept and validate**.

» Carefully balanced **constructive feedback** bridges the gap between over-praising (which might result in him being unrealistic or cocky) with under-praising (leaving him feeling incompetent).

» Use time alone to raise subjects such as **sex and pornography**. Do this well before you think your son may be sexually active.

» Make sure you know what you want to say before you launch in as you may not get many opportunities. Keep **revisiting tricky topics** whenever you can. Your opinions **matter** very much.

» Be **relaxed** about being physical – a hug in greeting or farewell, a touch or a friendly pat, or allowing a **closeness**, say while watching TV.

» **Healthy competition and fighting** between boys teaches them where the **limits** are by physically testing them (wounds, injury and even tears). Boys who have a brother will learn about **social bonding and friendship** through aggression. Dad can help a son develop healthy competition too.

» Make sure your son has opportunities to develop **good male friendships**.

TO SUM UP

In this book we have looked at what is going on behind the scenes in a teenager, at their personality tendencies, their needs, wants and detonation points and at the sort of parenting skills that work well for them during this period of transition.

What children need is to feel loved, be heard, feel motivated, have a sense of belonging and be optimistic about the future. What we do in terms of being a parent and what we offer in terms of the atmosphere in our family matter a lot. Good relationships with our children and family life itself, with all its ups and downs, go a long way towards creating a child who has a well-balanced sense of self and the confidence to function well as an adult. *The key tips on the next pages summarise the main themes in this book and we hope they will make life easier for you and your family.*

KEY TIPS FOR THE TEENAGE YEARS

» Recognise an emotional hijack and wait until calm before tackling the issue.

» Impose boundaries and limits in order to develop your child's resilience.

» Don't allow emotions to remain unexpressed.

» Be aware of self-regulation dials and detonation thresholds in your family.

» Demonstrate calm problem-solving. Try not to flap when things go wrong.

» Articulate and uphold your values so your child knows and understands them.

» Don't be afraid to apologise when necessary.

» Slowly loosen reins to encourage independence.

» Remember that behaviour is an effort to communicate a need.

» Think about which feelings are driving teenage behaviour.

» Infuse your family with warmth and an optimistic 'Yes I can' attitude.

» Listening and eye contact tops up emotional tanks.

» Be open, available, consistent and predictable in your approach.

» Communicate in a clear and straightforward way by saying what you mean.

» A good relationship with you improves your teenager's brain and their future relationships.

» Model what you want them to emulate as opposed to lecturing.

» Slowly change your communication to Adult-to-Adult mode.

- » Avoid overemphasis on punishments. Be firm and fair and offer warnings first.
- » Remember that addiction and motivation use the same pathways in the brain.
- » Keep an eye on your child's coping strategies and weak points.
- » Small changes in how you handle things can have a big impact on negative behaviour cycles in your family.
- » Discuss rather than lecture to encourage independent thinking and reflection.
- » Mistakes are an opportunity to change. Use constructive feedback to enable learning.

REFERENCES

CHAPTER 1

1. Goleman, D., *Emotional Intelligence*, Bloomsbury (London) (1996)
2. Damasio, A., *Descartes' Error: Emotion, Reason and the Human Brain*, Vintage (London) (2006)
3. Siegel, D. J., *The Developing Mind: How Relationships and the Brain Interact to Shape Who We Are*, 2nd ed. Guilford Press (New York) (2012)
4. Pert, C. B., *Molecules of Emotion: Why You Feel the Way You Feel*, Pocket Books (London) (1999)
5. MacLean, P. D., *A Triune Concept of the Brain and Behaviour*, University of Toronto Press (Toronto) (1973)

CHAPTER 2

1. Feinstein, S. G., *Secrets of the Teenage Brain: Research-based Strategies for Reaching and Teaching Today's Adolescents*, 2nd ed. Corwin/Sage Publications (Thousand Oaks) (2009)
2. Panksepp, J., *Affective Neuroscience: The Foundation of Human and Animal Emotions*, Oxford University Press (Oxford) (2004)
3. Moir, A. and; Jessel, D., *Brain Sex: The Real Difference Between Men & Women*, Mandarin (London) (1991)

CHAPTER 4

1. Dreikurs, R. and Stolz, V., *Children: The Challenge*, Plume (New York) (1992)
2. Bowlby, J., *A Secure Base*, Routledge Classics (London) (2005)

CHAPTER 8

1. See Chapter 4, Note 1
2. Bowlby, J., *The Making and Breaking of Affectional Bonds*, Routledge Classics (London) (2005)
3. Dreikurs Ferguson, E., *Adlerian Theory: An Introduction*, BookSurge Publishing (Charleston) (2009)
4. Berne, E., *Games People Play: The Psychology of Human Relationships*, Penguin (New York) (2010)

CHAPTER 9

1. Wilkins, P., *Person-centred Therapy: 100 Key Points*, Routledge (London) (2009)
2. Steiner, C. M., *Scripts People Live: Transactional Analysis of Life Scripts*, 2nd ed. Grove Press (New York) (1990)

FURTHER READING

PERSONALITY

Adler, A., *Understanding Life*, **Oneworld Publications (Oxford) (1997)** A clearly written guide to the psychologist's work, including his views on the development of personality.

Winnicott, D. W. and Winnicott, C., *Home is Where We Start From*, **Penguin (London) (1990)** Selected essays by a renowned psychoanalyst focusing on how a child's personality and mind develops in relation to family and environment.

GENDER DIFFERENCES

Apter, T., *Altered Loves: Mothers and Daughters During Adolescence*, **Harvester Wheatsheaf (Hemel Hempstead) (1990)** An examination of the mother–daughter relationship by a social psychologist, looking in particular at the pressures the relationship undergoes during adolescence. The book also suggests solutions and strategies to promote understanding and reconciliation.

Biddulph, S., *Raising Boys: Why Boys Are Different and How to Help Them Become Happy and Well-balanced Men*, **HarperThorsons (London) 2003** This practical guide by a family therapist underlines the distinctive needs of boys and lays out parenting strategies for the different stages of a boy's life.

Grant, I. and Grant, M., *Raising Confident Girls: Practical Tips for Bringing Out the Best in Your Daughter*, **Vermilion (London) (2009)** A practical book offering tools and techniques for parents to help them raise confident and communicative young women.

Kindlon, D. and Thompson, M., *Raising Cain: Protecting the Emotional Life of Boys,* **Random House (New York) (2000)** A thought-provoking book by child psychologists who examine the problems of many of today's boys – apathy, lack of empathy, poor communication, macho ideals – and highlight the part played in this by the destructive emotional training our boys receive. The book urges change to this miseducation and suggests ways of achieving this.

Sax, L., *Why Gender Matters: What Parents and Teachers Need to Know About the Emerging Science of Sex Differences,* **Harmony (New York) (2006)** A readable book on gender differences by a psychologist and physician, focusing on the different ways in which girls and boys think, feel and behave, and on the implications of this for the way in which we need to approach them.

Wiseman, R., *Queen Bees and Wannabes: Helping your Daughter Survive Cliques, Gossip, Boyfriends, and the New Realities of Girl World,* **Harmony (New York) (2009)** An insight into how girls operate and strategies to help you empower your daughter to deal better with friendships and conflicts.

OPTIMISM/RESILIENCE

Anderson, S., *Unbullyable,* **Good2gr8 Coaching (Buninyong) (2013)** Helpful in understanding the psychology of both persecutor and target and how to help children become emotionally robust and 'unbullyable'.

Bandura, A., *Self-efficacy: The Exercise of Control,* **Freeman (New York) (1997)** Although not directed at the general reader, this book written by a renowned psychologist gives an insight into why some people have a higher belief in their ability to achieve what they set out to and others don't.

Dweck, C., *Mindset: The New Psychology of Success,* **Robinson (London) (2012)** Drawing on widespread research and using extensive real-life examples, this very readable guide from a renowned Stanford psychologist explains why a positive mindset rather than talent alone is the key to success. The book also suggests how to achieve this outlook.

Seligman, M. E., *The Optimistic Child: A Proven Program to Safeguard Children Against Depression and Build Lifelong Resilience*, **Houghton Mifflin (Boston) (1995)** A renowned psychologist, Seligman advocates an approach to developing self-esteem and optimism that is based on mastering challenges, overcoming difficulties and experiencing individual achievement.

Seligman, M. E., *Learned Optimism: How to Change Your Mind and Your Life*, **Vintage (London) (2006)** Drawing on considerable research, Seligman offers techniques to enhance optimism and a positive way of viewing things.

Zolli, A. and Healy, A., *Resilience: Why Things Bounce Back*, **Simon & Schuster (New York) (2013)** An exploration of why some people are more resilient than others when things go wrong and what we can do to help our children learn how to bounce back from failure.

NEUROSCIENCE/NEUROBIOLOGY – HOW THE BRAIN/MIND WORKS

Church, D., *The Genie in Your Genes: Epigenetic Medicine and the New Biology of Intention*, **Energy Psychology Press (Fulton) (2009)** Corroborated by scores of research studies, Church argues that emotions – triggered by the emotional climate we experience – have the ability to turn genes on or off, concluding that emotions ultimately determine which genes (and therefore behaviours) are expressed and which ones lie dormant.

Cozolino, L., *The Neuroscience of Human Relationships: Attachment and the Developing Social Brain*, **W. W. Norton & Co. (New York) (2006)** Using diagrams and illustrations, Cozolino explains how brains are in fact highly social and try to connect with one another, influencing how they develop.

Morgan, N., *Blame My Brain: The Amazing Teenage Brain Revealed*, Walker (London) (2013) Accessible and well-researched examination of what goes on in the teenage brain.

Siegel, D., *Pocket Guide to Interpersonal Neurobiology*, W. W. Norton & Co. (New York) (2012) A lucid explanation of how our relationships shape our developing brain and mind, and the implications of this on personality.

Strauch, B., *Why Are They So Weird?*, Bloomsbury (London) (2004) An informative journey through the changes in the teenage brain.

PARENTING/EMOTIONAL INTELLIGENCE

Apter, T., *The Confident Child: Raising Children to Believe in Themselves*, W. W. Norton & Co. (New York) (2007) This readable book brings together considerable research into a guide on 'emotional coaching' – a way for parents to learn how to gauge and respond to a child's feelings so that children feel validated, valued and empowered.

Apter, T., *Difficult Mothers: Understanding and Overcoming their Power*, W. W. Norton & Co. (New York) (2012) Apter considers the power and influence of a mother and the different qualities mothers embody. She looks at the powerful impact of these on children, suggesting ways to overcome negative effects.

Dinkmeyer Sr, D., McKay, G. and Dinkmeyer Jr, D., *The Parent's Handbook*, Impact Publishers (Atascadero) (2007) A step-by-step programme with techniques for more effective parenting.

Elias, M., Tobias, S. and Friedlander, B., *Emotionally Intelligent Parenting*, Three Rivers Press (New York) (1999) Examines the strong role of emotion in the art of parenting and offers suggestions as to how to communicate with children at a deeper and more connected level.

Epstein, R., *The Case Against Adolescence: Rediscovering the Adult in Every Teen,* **Linden Publishing (Fresno) (2007)** Arguing that societies that don't think of the teenage years as a separate stage between child and adult have fewer problems with teenager misbehaviour, Epstein suggests that teens can and would be capable and responsible were they not treated like disruptive children and advocates giving them more responsibility at an earlier age.

Ginott, H., *Between Parent and Child,* **2nd ed. Crown Publications (New York) (2004)** This really helpful book shows readers how the skills of parenting can be learned.

Ginott, H., *Teacher and Child,* **Avon Books (1975)** This book was a classic of its time and helped adults develop better relationships with children through sound advice on communication and discipline.

Goleman, D., *Emotional Intelligence,* **Bloomsbury (London) (1996)** This groundbreaking book used developments in brain science (in mid 1990s) to provide evidence that our rational and decision making brain was dependent on our being able to manage our emotions. It argues that developing self-awareness, motivation, controlling impulses and empathy are the skills which accompany true happiness and success.

Gottman, J. and Declaire, J., *Raising an Emotionally Intelligent Child,* **Simon & Schuster (New York) (1998)** Using a five-step 'emotion coaching' process, this book helps parents to raise emotionally intelligent children who have an awareness of emotions in themselves and others.

James, O., *Love Bombing: Reset Your Child's Emotional Thermostat,* **Karnac Books (London) (2012)** A clearly explained self-help guide on how to recalibrate troubled relationships with children by connecting with them and resetting their emotional thermostat.

Skynner, R. and Cleese, J., *Families and How to Survive Them,* **Cedar Books (London) (1993)** Arranged as a conversation between Skynner (family therapist) and Cleese (client), this readable book touches on many of the issues that families face, from jealousy and fear to sadness and a teenager's quest for independence. The book offers discussion and practical advice on the issues it raises.

Steiner, C., *Achieving Emotional Literacy,* **Bloomsbury (London) (2001)** A step-by-step guide with practical exercises to improve emotional intelligence and literacy.

Winnicott, D. W., *The Child, the Family and the Outside World,* **Addison-Wesley, (Reading, MA) (1987)** An examination of basic childhood relationships by a renowned psychoanalyst who distinguishes parents' innate abilities from the parenting skills that need to be learnt.

THE EARLY YEARS

Gerhardt, S., *Why Love Matters: How Affection Shapes a Baby's Brain,* **Brunner-Routledge (Hove) (2004)** A persuasive and lively interpretation, corroborated by research in neuroscience, psychology and biochemistry, on why love is essential to social and emotional brain development in the early years.

Holmes, J., *John Bowlby and Attachment Theory,* **2nd ed. Routledge (London) (2014)** Invoking recent advances in biology and neuroscience, this accessible discussion by a leading psychiatrist examines Bowlby's concept of attachment between infant and caregiver. An understanding of infant attachment helps throw light on teenage separation anxiety.

Hudson Allez, G., *Infant Losses, Adult Searches,* **Karnac Books (London) (2009)** Arguing that the experience of the early years has a profound psychological impact on the child, this book shows how adverse circumstances can change brain structure and behaviour.

Sunderland, M., *What Every Parent Needs to Know*, Dorling Kindersley (London) (2007) An examination of the biochemical effects of how we love, nurture and play with our young children and the impact of this on their development.

Sunderland, M., *The Science of Parenting*, Dorling Kindersley, (London) (2008) Focusing on the early years, child psychotherapist Sunderland gives an overview of the science of different parenting styles and their effects on the child's brain development.

SELF-HARM

Levenkron, S., *Cutting: Understanding and Overcoming Self-mutilation*, Guilford Press (New York) (2006) Helpful in understanding the emotional roller coaster of self-harm, how these behaviours become habits and how to offer support.

Strong, M., *A Bright Red Scream: Self-mutilation and the Language of Pain*, Virago (London) (2005) Another informative account of the triggers to self-harm, why self-harm helps some people manage turbulent and unmanageable emotions, and how the self-destructive cycle can be broken.

THE CHANGING WORLD

Gerhardt, S., *The Selfish Society: How We All Forgot to Love One Another and Made Money Instead*, Simon & Schuster (London) (2010) An impassioned look at the disconnect between people in society today and a plea for the need to prioritise our emotional lives and connections above materialism.

Greenfield, S., *Tomorrow's People: How 21st-Century Technology is Changing the Way we Think and Feel*, Penguin (London) (2004) A wide-ranging and thought-provoking exploration of the possible implications of technology on our brains and personalities, and on how we think, feel and behave.

Sigman, A., *The Spoilt Generation: Why Restoring Authority Will Make Our Children and Society Happier*, Piatkus Books, (London) (2011) An accessible insight into what the author argues has gone wrong with this spoilt generation, how this has affected them and what adults can do to redress the balance and reclaim some of their lost authority.

COMMUNICATION

Harris, T. A., *I'm OK – You're OK*, Arrow Books (London) (1995) A clear and practical guide to Transactional Analysis, with explanations of how to move beyond predictable patterns of interaction.

Steiner, C. M., *Scripts People Live: Transactional Analysis of Life Scripts*, 2nd ed. Grove Press (New York) (1990) An illuminating look at life scripts, how they form early in life on the basis of the views of those around us and how they become a self-fulfilling prophecy as we live them out. The book also offers guidance on how to recognise and change our own life script.

Stewart, I. and Joines, V., *TA Today: A New Introduction to Transactional Analysis*, Lifespace (2012) A clear and practical introduction to the key concepts of communication in Transactional Analysis.

DISCIPLINE/PUNISHMENT

Nelsen, J. and Lott, L., *Positive Discipline for Teenagers: Empowering Your Teens and Yourself Through Kind and Firm Parenting*, 3rd ed. Three Rivers (New York) (2012) Psychologist and parent of seven, Nelsen elaborates on an approach to discipline that minimises the use of punishment and focuses instead on mutual respect, collaboration and firmness in managing behaviour.

Schafer, A., *Honey I Wrecked the Kids*, John Wiley (Mississauga) (2009) An easy read that looks at misbehaviour and parents' role in it, offering suggestions for how to improve behaviour management.

USEFUL RESOURCES

Counselling can be an effective part of a treatment programme if you are encountering problems. A good place to start your search for a therapist is either the British Association for Counselling & Psychotherapy (BACP) website (www.bacp.co.uk) for registered therapists or the **Counselling Directory** (www.counselling-directory.org.uk), which lists qualified therapists registered with any recognised organisation.

PARENTING

Family Journal – www.familyejournal.com
If communication between you and your teenager is flagging, this interactive US website provides an innovative online forum to make improvements.

Six Seconds – www.6seconds.org/tag/family
A US-based worldwide emotional intelligence network with lots of information on managing family and school life.

MENTAL HEALTH/DEPRESSION

Helpguide – www.helpguide.org
This US-based website gives information and help for parents in understanding and supporting a wide range of challenging mental-health issues.

James Wentworth-Stanley Memorial Fund – www.jwsmf.org
If you are concerned about your child slipping into depression,

this organisation provides support and information for parents and teenagers.

Tavistock and Portman NHS Trust – www.tavistockandportman. nhs.uk
NHS help for teenage mental-health issues (including depression) and addictions.

Young Minds – www.youngminds.org.uk
UK charity offering online support and advice on mental health for young people.

ALCOHOL ABUSE

Addaction – www.addaction.org.uk
Information, support and recovery programme for alcohol and drug dependency.

Drinkaware – www.drinkaware.co.uk
Information on the effects of alcohol and dependency, as well as useful facts about units, measures, etc. and a programme to support people in cutting down on their drinking. Also offers tips and advice for parents on how to approach conversations on alcohol with their children.

Hello Sunday Morning – www.hellosundaymorning.org
Promotes and supports a better drinking culture with more responsible alcohol use. Self-help website with a clear and structured programme with online support to reduce or stop alcohol consumption.

National Institute of Health – www.nih.gov
US government website with extensive information and research on the effects of drugs and alcohol on teenagers.

EATING DISORDERS (INCLUDING BULIMIA AND ANOREXIA)

Anorexia & Bulimia Care (ABC) – www.anorexiabulimiacare. org.uk
Provides advice and support to those affected by eating disorders, as well as to their families.

ANRED (Anorexia Nervosa and Related Eating Disorders) – www.anred.com
Information-based US website on eating disorders and how to initiate and support recovery.

Beat – www.b-eat.co.uk
Very informative website with information and help on all aspects of eating disorders. Offers helplines, online support, self-help groups, information booklets and recovery guides.

Counselling Directory – www.counselling-directory.org.uk/ eating.html
Directory of registered therapists specialising in anorexia, bulimia and other eating disorders.

NHS (Eating Disorders) – www.nhs.uk/conditions/eating-disorders
National Health Service website with information on the various eating disorders, as well as personal stories and NHS treatment options.

DRUGS (INCLUDING LEGAL HIGHS)

Addaction – www.addaction.org.uk
Information, support and recovery programme for drug and alcohol dependency.

Adfam – www.adfam.org.uk
Support organisation for alcohol and drugs users and their families.

Ceida – www.ceida.net.au
Australian site devoted to helping parents of younger children as well

as teenagers in understanding the dangers of drugs and keeping the lines of communication open with children.

Erowid – www.erowid.org
Online US information library containing detailed information on a wide range of drugs and their effects.

National Institute of Health – www.nih.gov
US government website with extensive information and research on the effects of drugs and alcohol on teenagers.

Talk to Frank – www.talktofrank.com
Information and support website for parents and children offering detailed information, with an A to Z list of substances (including legal highs) with explanations on how they are used, what they contain, their effects and their addictive qualities. Also lists the widely used slang terms and offers live chat online support as well as a telephone helpline.

SMOKING

A Choice 2 Live – www.achoice2live.com/know-your-addiction
Provides a detailed scrutiny of smoking as an addiction as well as suggestions on how to quit.

SELF-HARM

Counselling Directory – www.counselling-directory.org.uk/self-harm.html
Directory of registered therapists specialising in self-harm.

Harmless – www.harmless.org.uk
A user-led organisation providing information, support and training for those who self-harm, as well as for their families.

NHS (Self-harm) – www.nhs.uk/conditions/self-injury
National Health Service website with information and NHS treatment options.

National Self-harm Network (NSHN) – www.nshn.co.uk
Offers information and support with an online forum and phone helplines.

GAMBLING

Counselling Directory – www.counselling-directory.org.uk/gambling.html
Directory of registered therapists specialising in gambling problems.

Gambling Concern – www.gamblingconcern.org
NHS problem gambling clinic offering information and a treatment programme.

SCREEN ADDICTIONS

Counselling Directory – www.counselling-directory.org.uk/internet-addiction.html
Directory of registered therapists specialising in internet-based addictions.

Gaming Addiction – www.video-game-addiction.org
A US site focusing on teen gaming addiction. Provides information, resources and advice on treatment.

BULLYING

Bullying UK – www.bullying.co.uk
Advice and online support and forums on bullying (including cyber bullying).

COUPLES RELATIONSHIP PROBLEMS

College of Sexual and Relationship Therapists – www.cosrt.org.uk
Online information on personal relationships including gender issues, as well as a directory of therapists specialising in relationship issues.

Tavistock Centre for Couple Relationships – www.tccr.org.uk
Directory of therapists specialising in relationship difficulties.

ACKNOWLEDGEMENTS

We would like to thank all those who have helped through the ups and downs of a year dedicated to this project. Without the loyal and patient support of our husbands, Nick and Daniel, our children, Wiz, Bea, Ned, Claudia, Catriona, Alex and Sam, our parents and our friends, it would have been infinitely harder to have produced this book.

We would also like to thank Sam Jackson, our commissioning editor at Ebury Publishing, as well as Clare Hubbard our copyeditor, and Emma Kirby, our literary agent, whose enthusiasm and expertise has guided us through the publishing process. Also, thanks to Robert Duncan for his cartoon input. Thank you also to all the organisers and participants of our courses in the UK and overseas – the parents, staff and teenagers, whose shared experiences have helped to shape our ideas.

INDEX